Modern Riding

MODERN RIDING

by

Severyn R. Kulesza

SOUTH BRUNSWICK

NEW YORK: A. S. BARNES and CO., INC.

LONDON: THOMAS YOSELOFF LTD

©1966 by A. S. Barnes and Co., Inc.
Library of Congress Catalogue Card Number: 66-13062

A. S. Barnes and Co., Inc.
South Brunswick, New Jersey

Thomas Yoseloff Ltd
18 Charing Cross Road
London W.C. 2, England

First Printing, August 1965
Second Printing, December 1966

6398
Printed in the United States of America

Dedication

I bequeath the love of riding that the pages of this book contain to my four boys — Anthony, Andrew, Severyn and Hillary, and I dedicate this book not only to them, but to the youth of the world who will continue to enjoy the sport of riding as I have.

—S. Kulesza

Foreword

The last horse cavalry charge in the Western world took place when the Italian Brigade under Conte Bettoni charged the Russians at Stalingrad in 1944. After that the modern tank took over entirely and the age of the mounted horse cavalry in battle was dead. With it died a way of life which most of us think of as typified by gorgeous uniforms, daredevil feats of horsemanship, the clicking of heels in drawing rooms, and a whole series of subtle gradations in hand-kissing as gallant officers progressed from finger tips to palms to wrists to boudoirs.

Until I was introduced to Major Severyn Kulesza I had only books to tell me what life was like for these intrepid men of the saddle. Until I heard him speak of his life as a horseman and read the manuscript of this book I did not realize how much we could learn from the experience and training of a man for whom the science and art of equitation has been the one constant love of his life.

Major Kulesza is a man of middle height. His trim, youthful figure and erect bearing are expressive in every gesture of the military virtues by which he has lived. Every movement reveals an intense vitality, an undiminished stock of nervous energy. When he speaks, an expression humorous and ineradicably youthful lights up a face scored but not mutilated by experiences enough for more than one lifetime.

Born in Radom, seventy kilometers south of Warsaw, to a well-to-do family, Severyn R. Kulesza first learned to ride at the age of eight. His plans as an adolescent patriot to become a soldier in the newly-formed all-Polish units of the Polish Legion of Pilsudski were foiled when his sister betrayed his secret to his mother, who made him swear before the icon that he would not run away to carry them out. Not until three years later, in 1918, when he was eighteen, was he finally able to become a recruit in the Polish Lancers. This time his mother accompanied him to the station, where he boarded the train with the other recruits. As the train was about to depart, a railway signalman solemnly made the sign of the cross with his signal lamp, Severyn's mother fainted, and the trainload of recruits went off to war. Later, in the parcel which his mother had packed for him, he found his first bottle of vodka, and knew, as he puts it, that he had truly been promoted a soldier.

Major Kulesza's service as a cavalry officer spanned two major world wars, during which he won the Virtuti Militari, Poland's highest medal for valour, equivalent to the British Victoria Cross. In the inter-war years he devoted himself to the science of horsemanship. A superb rider, he won many individual competitions and led his teams to victory in many others. Among his outstanding victories were: the Silver Medallion, Olympic Games, for his team in 1936, two (individual) championships of Poland in three day events, one championship in dressage, three vice championships during six successive years during which he came either first or second, and several international first prizes.

Three-time-winner of the President Cup of Poland, Major Kulesza's fondest riding memory is of the President Cup Jumping Competition of 1930, when a fair stranger at the track showed exceptional understanding of a cavalry of-

ficer's superstitious nature. When he approached the young
lady with profuse apologies for daring to accost her without
formal introduction, the only excuse that Severyn Kulesza
could offer was that the competition which he was about to
enter was uppermost in his mind and that only she could
assure his victory. It speaks well for the sporting spirit of
the ladies of Poland that she allowed him the small liberty
on which he felt that his victory depended. With what
difficulty she overcame her modest reserve can well be
imagined, but gamely she lifted up her skirt there at the
crowded track and allowed the gallant rider to fling himself
down on the turf and kiss her left knee. It is surprising that
he carried off both first and second prizes that year, not to
speak of the brief but unforgettable friendship of his bene-
factress?

He became widely known in his native land. Indeed,
when he was on the run and physically ill after the defeat of
the Polish Army by the Germans in 1939, and working his
way through the German lines back to Warsaw, peasants
and townspeople who recognized him took unwanted risks
to nurse him back to health and help him on his way. His
eventual capture by the Germans no doubt had something
to do with the fact that it was not easy for him to fade to
anonymity even in civilian clothes.

When the war and his imprisonment were over, Severyn
Kulesza emerged into a new world, a world in which the
horse cavalry no longer existed. Shaken in confidence after
his lengthy ordeal, he was uncertain of his future and that
of his beloved vocation in a mechanized world. But his
reputation had not faded during his long period of enforced
idleness. It was at this point that he was invited to England,
where a master trainer was urgently needed who could
supervise the training of the horses which were to take part
in the public ceremonials related to the wedding and later

the coronation of Her Majesty, Queen Elizabeth II of England. As the guards at Hyde Park Barracks snapped to attention for him, he knew that he was once again in a world where his unique skills were invaluable. Within a year and eight months he and his hand-picked team of aides had trained 120 horses, at London and Windsor, in that faultless precision and beauty of performance which were later to dazzle the spectators.

Now Major Kulesza has performed an invaluable service to lovers of equitation by setting down so entertainingly, for our pleasure and instruction, these ground rules of his craft. Luckily, he is a born raconteur, with the rare gift of bringing an experience to life by evoking for the listener or the reader the sensations associated with it. His memory is filled not only with what was, but with the feel of how things were. This is the gift of the born story teller who, with an amused and passionate detachment, can make of the details of his own life a work of art in retrospect. It is a gift which an artist might well envy.

How does one maneuver one's way through a narrow strip of no-man's land between the Russian and the German armies in dead of night, without falling into the hands of either army? Severyn Kulesza did it and swears he smelled his way between them. Every army, he explains, has its own characteristic smell. The Russian Army smell is compounded of bad tobacco, the tar from boot blacking, and cabbage soup. The German Army smells of coffee, leather, better tobacco, and sweat. It's not so hard to survive if you have finely attuned senses.

It is not surprising, then, that the Major begins this handbook of modern riding with a description of the sense equipment of the horse, of how the horse perceives and how it responds to what it perceives. It is clear that he understands, as a result of long experience and study, and by a form of natural empathy, the responses of the horse, their causes and their significance. I once heard an admirer of his say, "It's uncanny. He thinks like a horse." True. And of course, he thinks like a human being too, which is perhaps why such a man can tell us more about the human-horse relationship and what it should be than anyone else.

Major Kulesza is concerned with the crucial question, how to get the maximum pleasure and efficiency out of the union of horse and person in equitation, without violating the natural physical integrity of either. He is an outspoken exponent of a horse-rider relationship shorn of artificial elements which hamper both and pervert the natural beauty of their functioning. He objects frankly to that which is uncomfortable or unnatural for either. You may or may not agree with his opinions on high dressage, for instance, but in either case you will find them illuminating. And you cannot fail to find them entertaining, as the Major is throughout, even when he is most precisely technical. A phrase here or a reminiscence there brings an era to life; people we'd like to know more about live again briefly, and even horses reveal their individuality as we come to understand them more intimately. We discover the value of getting to know not just what a horse is, but who the individual horse is, and we begin to appreciate what riding can be like when the horse is a companion who is also enjoying himself.

This book accomplishes many things, some of them for the first time. It is that rare item, at present as far as I know non-existent in English, a succinct but comprehensive handbook of equitation. Like all expressions of mastery, it is dazzlingly simple. It is logical and simple with the logic and simplicity of perfected art. The veteran rider and trainer cannot fail to appreciate and profit by the logic and insight which Major Kulesza reveals. Riders in every stage of development will find here invaluable pointers for the increase of skill and enjoyment. Even armchair riders will take pleasure in this intimate and humane description of the ideal relationship between man and horse. They will not only end up convinced that they too would love to learn to ride, but are in danger of being deluded by the perfectly simple and apparently self-evident instructions into feeling that they can already do so.

It is not too risky to venture to predict that this handbook into which Major Kulesza has been prevailed upon to pour the distilled essence of a lifetime's experience, will prove to be a classic of its kind.

ADELE WISEMAN

Preface

I am not sure whether it was coincidence or providence which brought me after many, many years of wandering all over the world to Winnipeg, Canada. I was invited to come by Mr. George Andison, the father of a charming girl who was my pupil during Summer of 1962 in Phoenix Hall Farm, Ontario. I will be grateful to him as long as I live, because thanks to him, I found myself in the heart of Canada, in the capital city of Manitoba—the country where once upon a time Indians chased the buffaloes across the vast prairies, where the horizon reaches probably the end of the world and the sun as it sets throws its last rays in a scheme of colours which seem to me an everlasting miracle.

Here I found myself amongst extremely kind people, whose hearts are as large as the prairies and whose thinking as vast as the horizon of Manitoba. I found myself amongst the lovers of the horse and riding. But I met for the first time in my life ideas of riding which we Europeans would consider a little bit "Archaic." There I discovered one rides two ways—"Western" and "English" and by English one means any way of riding which differs from the riding of the cowboy.

My lessons and particularly my lectures seemed to provide a great interest in a "new" direction.

13

One evening before Christmas, 1962, Mr. George Sellers suggested that I should try to write a book.

"Try," he said, "to write as you lecture."

Mrs. Sellers, a charming and extremely talented person with great enthusiasm for the education of the youth and the future of Canada in all spheres, like ballet, art gallery, symphonic orchestra, theatre, etc., offered to help me with the writing of this book.

Here I would like to express my deepest gratitude to these two people whose faith and assistance have made this book a reality.

To Mrs. Sellers I offer special appreciation. She not only corrected my "Penglish" (Polish-English, as she calls it) but she sacrificed her time and energy to force me to write, and each part that I wrote, to re-write with her every week. Also, she encouraged me (maybe she was wrong) to illustrate my writings, with my "scribbles" which I have done during our conversations. All the sketches are original except the diagram of the muscles, which I took from the book of my friend, Major Krolikiewicz, *The Rider and the Horse at the Jump and the Cross Country*.

Also, the gaits of the horse I copied from the book of Ludwig Koch, *Die Reitkunst im Bilde*. Otherwise, the book is written without any other sources of reference for help, except from my own memory and experience.

I have tried to explain the principles of the modern way of riding in a popular way to the benefit of all readers. This book is simply a verbal and pictorial illustration of my teaching. It is my hope that it will appeal to the youngsters as well as the more advanced riders. Perhaps it will even help to raise the level of riding. Who knows—for such is the goal of any instructor.

S. KULESZA

Contents

Introduction

When I was a prisoner of war, I was asked by my cavalry friends to give a lecture on how I visualized riding as a sport in future years. Well, I must admit that at that time I was very pessimistic. We all know that riding as an international sport used to be held in the hands of the cavalry man in all countries. In the modern battlefield there is no place for horses or horsemen. The last cavalry charge took place in Russia during the period of the Stalingrad operation in 1944, at which time the Italian cavalry brigade under the leadership of the late Count Bettoni, a famous international rider before the war, charged the Russians. The cavalry of all modern armies dismounted horses and "mounted" tanks or armored cars. Mechanization superseded the horse all over the world.

How could I expect that in spite of this, and moreover, in spite of this period of atomic explosions and all sorts of "sputniks," that riding as a sport would develop and grow to such an extent as witnessed today? More and more people, and particularly young girls and ladies, want to ride horseback.

Jumping competitions and the three day[1] and one day[2] events have developed even more than before the war. I think that the more mechanized life becomes, the greater desire people have to get closer to nature. And who will provide a better means than our noblest animal, the horse— a well-trained horse! I do not believe there is any other sport which gives more pleasure and excitement than riding cross-country. When galloping fast across rough difficult country, the horse goes as though without a rider, easily, freely and carefully, using himself in his natural way to avoid all obstacles. The rider in full harmony with the animal adapts himself to the natural movements of his mount, both co-operating and sharing a mutual confidence in each other. These two creatures have their own wills, brains, faculties, reactions, but they become as one, like a modern centaur. The rider gives the orders and leaves it to his horse to execute them.

In other words: The rider's business is—"what to do."

The horse's business is—"how to do it."

As soon as the rider feels that the horse understands his order, he permits him to carry it out. To facilitate this, the rider tries to follow the movements of the horse with as little interference as possible. *This is the principle of modern*

[1] Three day event—the object of this test is an endeavour to prove the degree of endurance of a really good charger or hunter, which has been well-trained and brought to a state of excellent condition. At the same time, it is a test of the rider's knowledge of pace and the use of his horse across country. First day—dressage test; Second day—endurance test; about 22 miles in 5 phases completed without a break; Third day—jumping over course in jumping arena.

[2] One day event—preliminary test to three day event. Dressage test and jumping test as in the three day event. Instead of the second day's endurance test, there is only the fourth phase—the cross country.

Mlle. Francoise Vanderhagen, twice champion of Belgium, going over a 7′ wall in International show at Ostend. Note the impeccable style of horse and rider; again the lightness of hands and correct position of the leg.

(Photo—Dobrski, Brussels)

riding. Then will be achieved the economy of work, *the maximum result with the minimum effort,* which produces the proper style.

As in all other sports, i.e., tennis, golf, skiing, we must first of all achieve proper style. We must know how to use our movements economically to obtain the best results. After this comes the question of pure enjoyment, competing, and winning. However, there is not a single instructor in the world who can inject into his pupils the will to win. This must be innate. If the rider has no inborn competitive spirit and no ambition to win, he is not for competition. I remember this from my own experience. I was trained to be a riding instructor in our cavalry school of equitation. I was very conscientious about riding with the impeccable style which I achieved. But I did not win often. I completed many "parcours" without faults, but rarely received a first prize. One day in 1929 during an international competition in Poznan, riding three horses, I did not touch a fence but I was placed eighth. Cross with myself, I asked our best rider at that time, an authority, Major Antoniewicz, "Tell me, what is wrong with my riding? Why can't I win?" He said, "Because you do not want to win. You think too much about your style and not enough about speed. Forget about it, your style is there. Go in and think about winning." And that was the truth.

We went to Warsaw, our biggest international show. On the first day I was first, tied with Captain Leguio, the best Italian rider and an Olympic winner in 1920. The second day I won the speed competition (parcour de chasse). The third day I placed third.

There are many very good riders who never win because of the lack of will to do so. There are also many excellent competitors, winners, who do not bother about good style. I believe there are too many competitors who ride very badly; rough riders whose principle is—It does not matter how I ride, I must win. And, mounted on outstanding jumpers, they win very often in spite of ugly riding.

Of course, in competition it is not enough to ride beautifully, but I cannot understand why a good competitor could not and should not endeavour also to have perfect style. Believe me, it is not so very difficult to be correct. One must only follow some principles of *equitation*. Now, somebody might ask what I mean by "equitation." Is it just riding, any riding, or is it some special sort of riding?

I would say that any way of using a horse's four legs instead of our own two legs as a means of transportation from A to B we can call riding, providing we sit on the horse's back. But equitation is something more. It is knowledge and a science based on years of experience and study of the horse as an animal and as an engine working with the rider in total co-operation. Thanks to this knowledge, the great masters of equitation created the methods of training the horse and rider *according to the purposes of the time*.

Before the last world war every country had its own cavalry. Each cavalry had its own centre of equitation where the best instructors not only trained the rider and the horse, but also did the research necessary to create the best method for its cavalry. I was fortunate to be attached for eight years to our Polish Cavalry School in Grudziadz as an instructor and Commanding Officer of instructors' courses. At the same time I was a member of our International Jumping Team and three-day event team, which took part in the Olympic games in Berlin in 1936. As a result, I had the opportunity of studying and of taking part in the riding research work.

To establish a method of riding most suitable for our

Myself, as a Captain competing in International show jumping competition in Nice in 1933. Note the correct position of leg and the relaxed hands following the natural movement of the head and neck.

army's purpose at that time, we had to take under consideration:

(1) The maximum time allowed by the army authorities to have the rider and horse ready for war;

(2) The character, temperament and mentality of the rider. (For example, there is a great difference between the German Character and the Polish one, or between the Italian and French, as is reflected in their methods of training.)

(3) The temperament, character and breeding of our horses;

(4) The conditions, such as climate, configuration, etc., of the country.

I remember our recruits joined the regiment in the middle of October. At the beginning of February our winter maneuvers were scheduled. The recruits had to be ready for them. The time we had at our disposal was therefore only from the last two weeks of October until the end of January. There were three or four riding lessons in a week. There were about fourteen weeks; in other words, that meant approximately forty-five riding lessons. And so, the method of teaching had to be very clever and adapted to these stringent demands,—differing from the ideas of the time when a soldier in the cavalry served four years. Therefore, the method had to be simplified for the rider as well as for the horse.

In 1926 new methods for both riding instruction and instruction for training the horse were introduced in our cavalry. Both were based on the modern principles originated by the great Italian, Captain Frederico Caprilli. This master of modern equitation, this great genius, rider, and instructor, died fifty years ago. His influence has been felt in all countries where riders try to ride over jumps and cross-country according, more or less, to his principles. Unfortunately his sound and "nearest to the truth" ideas are very often distorted by misunderstanding, wrong interpretation, and lack of proper training.

Also, there are people who try to combine two ideas of riding which are basically different; one is train the horse and rider in old-fashioned methods of the 19th century which we call "dressage," and the other is to jump, but only jump following the natural system of Caprilli.

To explain more clearly the difference between these two ideas, I will quote my own letter which was published in *Horse and Hound* in October, 1949.

Where the idea is to develop to the maximum the natural abilities of the horse to cross rough country and negotiate fences of all kinds, the "Caprilli" system is unsurpassed, because without interfering with the natural balance of the horse and without destroying his initiative, this system develops, to the highest degree, the collabroation and the co-operation between horse and rider, which is indispensible if they are to cross a country safely and to the best advantage.

It must, however, be particularly remembered that the whole idea of the Caprilli system is that the horse should be really obedient and disciplined, with great confidence in his rider. This entails as a preliminary measure, the standard or ordinary training, known at the moment as "elementary dressage."

I would like to elaborate slightly on the difference between so-called "elementary dressage" and the really advanced dressage and high school. Elementary dressage does not entail "collecting the horse" in the usual accepted sense of the word. It consists only of natural movements. The "dressage" system proper educates the horse in an entirely different way, because the rider by collecting him to a marked degree, gives him an artificial balance and an even different silhouette. The neck is raised and shortened because it is never stretched in a natural way to assist his balance over fences. The hind quarters are lowered and drawn artificially under his body. All his movements are constricted. It is obvious then that "advanced dressage" tends to destroy the natural initiative of the horse, because the rider controls and dictates every step he takes. The animal gradually becomes something of an automaton and loses his capacity to think for himself and to adapt his balance to any unexpected situations in which he may find himself.

In the Caprilli system, the horse is taught to balance himself and the rider adjusts his seat (*or better let us call it his position*) to all the animal's actions. This system cannot teach artificial movements such as "passage,"[1] "piaffe,"[2] "levade,"[3] etc., of the high school, or even the extreme collection required by the movements of advanced dressage. These movements are now only an art—a very real art in themselves. They have no relation to every day utility. This is because they were originated and developed in the epoch of hand-to-hand combat, which has long since faded into the past. They remain with us as a charming, interesting, and most highly skilled reminder of the art of horsemanship in those bygone times.

On the other hand, Caprilli's system was originally a method of traning the comparatively modern cavalry trooper, who might often be ordered to cross some difficult country alone in the course of his duty. It is therefore evidently suitable for modern individual riding and sport of all kinds, whether steeple-chasing, hunting, or show-jumping.

The creators of the previously-mentioned Polish instruction, Colonel J. Kossak, our chief instructor at that time, and Captain L. Kon, our best instructor and, in my opinion, the best judge of riding in the world, based their work on the principles of Italian natural equitation. Gradually through years of experience we followers improved upon it, adding some new ideas to achieve the same result more rapidly. I was always studying the same problem: how to facilitate the method of training riders and horses, particularly in our modern post-war times when people have insuf-

---

[1] passage—highly collected trot. The horse slows down the rhythm and lifts his legs higher than at the ordinary trot. He uses his pushing energy more up than forward. He lifts his knees nearly up to the height of his chest.

[2] piaffe—a sort of trot on the spot.

[3] levade—rearing movement at the command of the rider, during which the horse remains on his hind legs for designated period.

ficient riding time, patience, or money for too many lessons. I have endeavored to improve these methods, thus making it easier and quicker to achieve the maximum results in the minimum time.

This method I would compare with "Basic English." During the war, professors of the English language developed a method to make the teaching of English simpler and faster for the foreigner to learn. This basic method consisted of the most important principles of grammar, some elocution and necessary spelling, as well as a vocabulary of 800 words.

It is the same with this method of riding. We acquire the necessary knowledge of how to control the horse and how to adapt ourself in a natural way to the movements of the horse, and how to train our horse in the easiest way.

I have had pupils who after a course of 40 lessons were ready to ride cross-country, out hunting, or to participate in small show jumping, of course on a reasonably well-trained horse. I also have had beginners who could learn to ride and at the same time to train their novice horses. Both have made extraordinarily quick progress. *Believe me, there is no mystery*.

Somebody asked the famous Polish pianist, Paderewski, whether it was difficult to play the piano. His answer was: "Not very difficult. One has only to know which finger to put on which key, and for how long. That is all. And then practice for six hours daily. I will try to explain—which finger and for how long to put it on which key. We will try to play, not necessarily symphonies, but nice simple songs which will penetrate into your heart and help you to enjoy life."

Modern Riding

PART I.
THE HORSE

1.

The Horse As an Engine from the Rider's Point of View

As we mentioned in our introduction, the main principle of modern riding consists of *co-operation between the rider and the horse, in full confidence for each other.*

The horse will have confidence in his rider—

(1) When he has the feeling that the rider will never ask him to do the impossible, nor ask him to do something which he is unable to perform either because of limited physical ability, or because he is unprepared to do it through lack of training or understanding;

(2) when he knows that the rider will give him clear orders at the right moment, and then let him act;

(3) when he feels that the rider through co-operation will help him to act.

The rider will have confidence in his horse, when he

33

knows how much he can expect from him because of his qualities, such as courage, stamina, and standard of training. So, to ride properly according to this principle, which means to give the orders to the horse correctly, clearly and at the right moment, and to help him, we must have some knowledge about the horse as a sort of engine working under our weight. We must therefore understand the structure of our animal and his psychology. It is not of great importance to know how many bones and muscles the horse has. However, if we are to co-operate fully with him, we must know and understand the parts of his structure which play an important role.

LEGS The body of the horse is suspended on four pillar-like legs, but the pillars are not built the same way.

The front legs are attached to the body by means of muscles and tendons in the shoulders, and are not fixed. There are no articulations in connection with the spine. The body is supported as though on strings between the shoulders and the part A-B of the leg serves as a sort of crutch. This part is straight when supporting the body and doing the main job. The movement of the front leg is very limited. By their very shape and their manner of working, they were created by nature to *support the horses' body*. This is their function; they do not create movement. The dotted line C-D illustrates the range of movement of the front legs.

The hind legs are built differently. First of all they are attached to the body by very strong articulations in the pelvic bones, which are firmly connected with the spine. The legs are never straight when supporting the hind part of the body; they are straightened when they give the push. The dotted line E-F illustrates the range of movement of the hind legs. The fact that these strong bones are connect-

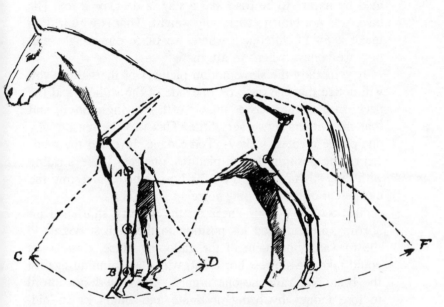

Fig. 1 Illustrating the range of movement of the horse's legs.

ed by strong articulations, proves that nature created the
hind legs, together with the pelvic bones, as the engine
which creates movement. The hind quarters *push* and throw
the horse's body forward, and the front legs accept and
take it, thus supporting the whole body of the horse. The
front legs, in co-operation with the movement of the neck,
also help to give the horse's spine the elevation necessary
to create the moment of suspension when the horse is
above the ground. All the power of the push is transferred
to the front by the muscles and by the movement of *the
back*.

BACK To ride on horseback we have to place ouselves one way or another on the horse's *back*. The horse was created by nature to be free, like a stag, a deer, or a fox. His back was not built to carry any weight. That is why it does make a lot of difference where we place our weight and how we behave when we are there.

If you study the slow motion pictures of the gallop, you will notice that the back on one side of the withers and the neck on the other moves in sort of a swaying motion, and that the withers move very little. This was the reason why one of the greatest jockeys, Tod Sloane, invented the modern racing position. In old pictures, one sees jockeys riding with long stirrups, seated on the horse's back, arresting the movement of the galloping horse .

Tod Sloane put his knees on the withers, shortened his stirrups, and adapted his position to the highest degree to the forward movement of the galloping horse. Result—he could take the slowest horse and win when running against the best. Naturally no-one argued. One could not afford to lose money by being obstinate and riding in an old-fashioned, impractical way. Since then, the jockey has changed his seat. In flat races the rider does not use his legs to push his horse. His stirrups are too short, and the legs are placed too far in front of the horse's body. He simply places his weight over the horse's center of gravity and moves with the natural movement of the neck. The idea is to help the horse to balance himself forward and to "catch" the ground as much as possible.

For ordinary riding across difficult country we cannot ride this way, but we must follow the same idea, which is *to facilitate the work of the horse's back*. That means, we should not sit as was done in the Middle Ages, on the two bones in our seat. We should touch the saddle with our seat as lightly as we can, and as soon as the horse needs to

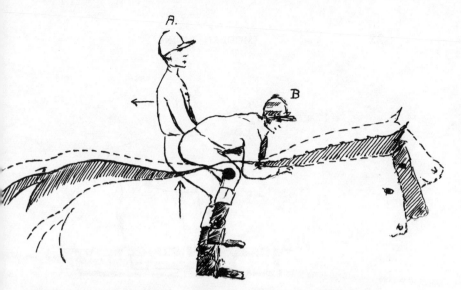

Fig. 2 Illustrating the difference between the "A" old fashioned and "B" modern position of the jockey.

have his back free, we do it by adopting a *half seat,* which puts us in the balance line of the horse. When training a young horse, a heavy seat in the saddle causes objection, which the horse shows by arching and stiffening his back. And so to be rid of the unpleasant weight of the rider, he bucks very often. (For details on training in the half-seat, see PART II—The Rider.)

HEAD AND NECK The head and neck play the same role in a horse's movements as the hands of human beings. We do not like to be handcuffed, particularly when running, or walking on slippery or rough ground. We balance ourselves by using our hands. The horse uses his head and neck to balance himself.

In the second half of the 18th century, two French veterinarians and horsemen, Goubaux and Barrier, published

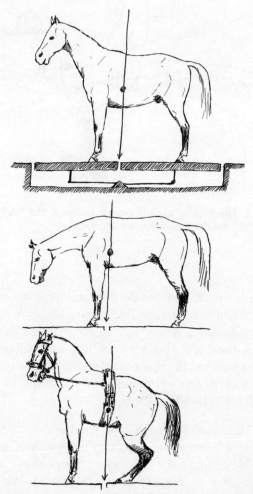

Fig. 3 Illustrating (A) natural balance, (B) neck down, balance forward, (C) neck shortened and raised or hind legs under, balance line back.

their book about the horse, in which they explained their experiments dealing with the balance of the horse. A hundred years later, Bausher and Morris repeated the same experiment. I, myself, with our veterinarian, Colonel Wroblewski, also repeated the same experiment for the sake of experience.

By using a special scale, we weighed the horse, putting the hind legs on one side of the scale and the front legs on the other. By moving the horse forward or back we levelled the scale. It showed that the true balance is exactly where the withers ends. That means the balance line falls nearer to the front legs. The weight of horse's body is distributed on his four legs in this way: about two-thirds is on front legs and about one-third on the hind legs. When the rider places himself in the right position on the horse's back, his weight is distributed in the same proportion. Naturally it is so when the horse stands squarely on four legs and the neck and head are in the natural position of attention. But when the head and neck are lowered and stretched forward, the point of gravity moves forward. If you make the horse raise his neck and flex his head so that his neck will shorten, the point of gravity moves back.

When the horse is forced to place his hind legs under his body, he lowers his hindquarters slightly, and the point of gravity moves back. If we stretch the hind legs a little or put the horse's hind legs slightly higher, the point moves forward. This proved that the co-ordination of the movement between the neck and the hindquarters balances the horse according to his necessity. The faster the horse goes, the more he pushes his point of gravity forward in front of his front legs, to force them to "catch" the ground and prolong what we might call the basis of his balance. When the horse wants to have natural balance he regulates it by co-ordinating the movement of the neck in conjunction with the movement of the hindquarters. For example, when the horse lies down, he lowers his neck to the ground. At the same time he draws his hind legs under his body, thus lowering his hindquarters. The point of gravity is, in its natural place, nearer to the front legs. He then bends one of his front legs, and depending on which side he wants to lie down, falls to the ground. This shows what an important role the head and neck play in keeping the horse's body in natural balance. This is so particularly in movements over rough country and jumps.

Therefore, it is understandable that it must irritate and upset the horse, when the rider does not permit him to use his neck and head freely (in a natural way) in moments of natural effort to overcome difficulties when going over rough country.

Let us realize that the rider uses his hands to control the speed and direction of the horse. He attaches his hands by means of the reins and the bit to the horse's mouth which is the most delicate and sensitive point of the horse as our engine.

Try to put yourself in the horse's position.

Very often ignorant people put a cold and sometimes sharp, very thin bit in the mouth of a young sensitive animal. This unpleasant bit very often causes him pain. Naturally, rather than gaining confidence, it arouses suspicion, and as a result the desire to get rid of this unpleasant object is established. Trouble starts when the rider tries to connect the badly trained hands with the horse's mouth. The horse starts to fight the hands, either by raising his head and contracting his neck, or by overbending and thus going "behind the bit," as people usually call this kind of escape on the part of the horse. Or, the horse loses his temper and tries to escape from this discomfort by running away. One can understand why the proper introduction of the bit in the mouth is very important. It is essential to examine the shape of the mouth and then to introduce the proper snaffle, which at the beginning should be thick, plain, or even rubber. Very often the horse uses his tongue to help himself loosen the pressure of the bit. Some horses contract the tongue and press it against the bit, some slip the tongue over the bit, open the mouth and throw the tongue out on one side of the mouth. I am pointing out all the difficulties one can avoid if one introduces, in a proper manner, the weight of the rider on the horse's back and the hands of the rider in relation to the mouth, the head, and neck.

It is also very important to look at the place where the head and neck of the horse are connected. If this connection is thick and heavy, the horse is inclined to stiffen his jaw and will consequently raise his head and neck in self-defence. When it is light, the horse is inclined to overbend, and try sometimes to avoid pressure by shaking his head up and down. There are many different ways that the horse defends himself against the bit. The good rider can avoid this by applying the proper bit and introducing the hands in the correct way.

The above mentioned shows the great importance of the proper treatment of the head and neck of the horse by the rider, because these parts of the horse's anatomy are the sources of all the difficulties in training and riding.

MUSCLES The horse uses himself *instinctively*. The movements are produced by his muscles. And here I would like to mention groups of muscles which, when interfered with by the rider, spoil the co-ordination of the natural movements of the horse. In training a jumper or hunter these muscles play an extremely important role.

Here again I do not want to elaborate the whole muscle system in the horse's body as is done for veterinary students.

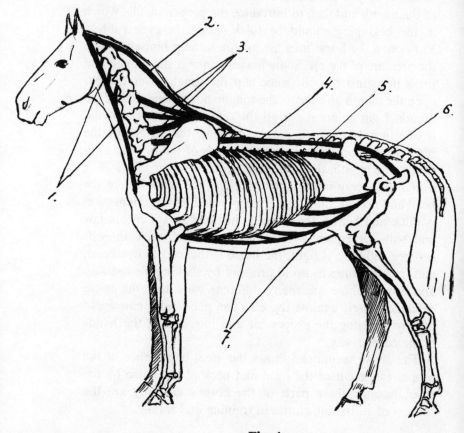

Fig. 4

I would like only to draw the attention of my readers to some muscles or groups of muscles which should be developed, exercised, and left free to execute their functions if we want the horse to move economically under the rider across difficult country and over jumps.

As I mentioned before, the neck is the most important balancing factor in the natural movements of the horse. Therefore I would like to point first to the three groups of muscles of the neck, which on the diagram are numbered 1, 2, and 3. The co-operation between these muscles moves the head and neck up and down, and also stretches and shortens the neck.

Muscle No. 1 is a double muscle which runs from the top of the horse's scalp to the joint of the shoulder, and is also attached to the lower parts of the first vertebrae of the neck. This muscle moves the neck down and also moves the shoulder joint forward, helping the front leg to step out. We can see the importance of the proper functioning of these muscles for a jumper who must use his neck over fences.

Muscles No. 2 and No. 3 are the two groups of neck muscles which keep the neck in the proper position. Muscles No. 2 are attached at one end to the horse's head and at the other to the withers. Muscles No. 3 are like a fan, one end attached to the upper parts of the last vertebrae of the neck and the other end attached to the inside of the shoulder blades. This muscle on the one hand holds the shoulders to the horse's body, and on the other supports the neck and keeps it in its proper position.

Next is *Muscle No. 4*—the longest muscle of the horse's back. On one end it is attached to the seventh vertebrae of the neck and at the other is attached to the upper part of the hips. Those muscles are also attached to all vertebrae along the horse's back above the spine.

Muscle No. 6 prolongs muscle No. 4. It is attached to the bone of the hips at one end and at the other to the upper part of the bones of the thighs. This muscle is used in all the horse's movements, when he pushes his body forward by straightening the articulation of the hips.

As a sort of opposition to those groups of muscles, is *Muscle No. 5* which runs under the spine and is attached to all the vertebrae in their lower parts and to the upper parts of the bone of the thigh. This muscle bends the end of the horse's spine and pulls the hindquarters under the horse's body.

The group of *Muscles No. 7* works also as opposition to muscles No. 4 and 6. These muscles are attached to the chestbone on one end, and to the pelvis bone and hip bones on the other. The horse uses these muscles when he takes his hind legs under his body.

It is easy to understand how important it is to develop all these muscles during the training of a young jumper and cross country horse, if we want him to work to the best advantage. Therefore in modern riding we introduce the horse to a whole system of exercises over cavaletti and jumps, as well as climbing up and down hills. Understanding the role of the above mentioned muscles in the natural movements of the horse, particularly over obstacles, we can see that collecting the horse in the old fashioned manner *interferes with his economy of action,* and that is why we leave him in his natural balance and we adapt ourselves to his movements, interfering with him as little as possible.

HEART AND LUNGS When buying a horse we can easily see if he is well shaped, but we are unable to see his heart and lungs at a glance. These are perhaps the most important parts of the horse working as an engine under our weight. I do not want to discuss biology *at great length,* rather I would like to draw a parallel between the engine of a car and the body of a horse.

The car must have all the working parts of its engine in place, well adjusted, and must have the necessary fuel to produce the required power. The engine has a pump which delivers the gas; the magnet delivers the spark which creates the explosion, which in turn moves the pistons, and so on. similarly, the horse has nerves which correspond to the explosions of the mixture of gas and air in the car. The nerves cause the action of the muscles, as they shorten and stretch. The nerve centre is, of course, in the brain. By shortening and stretching, the muscles move the bones which execute the various movements that have been described above. The muscles get their nourishment, such as the essential vitamins, through the lungs and stomach. The necessary oxygen is supplied through the skin and lungs. The heart pumps the oxygen through the blood, supplying the nerves and muscles. The carbon dioxide is removed from the body through the blood stream, the lungs, the sweat of the horse, and other excretions.

In freedom, the horse regulates his work and the speed of his movements instinctively according to the strength of his heart. He cannot gallop faster than the lungs can receive oxygen and throw away carbon dioxide. In other words, the horse cannot work faster or harder than the heart can pump blood. Throughout training, the co-ordination between the heart, lungs, and muscles is developed. Through ignorance we can hurt the heart of the horse by asking more of him than he is able to give. That is why I suggest, when buying a horse it does not matter how pretty and "darling" he is. Ask a good veterinarian to examine his heart carefully, especially when buying a horse from the race track.

One of my best pupils in Brussels, M. Velge, bought a lovely grey Thoroughbred, an excellent mover with good temperament. He jumped very well and powerfully, but there were days when he refused any jump. It did not matter what size the fence was. The previous owners probably forced him to jump without asking why suddenly he refused. Even from afar he stopped and would not go to the same fence which he had jumped a day before without any trouble. I watched him carefully and I noticed that when he refused, his heart beat very distinctly. The more we forced him the more he showed fright. I watched him in the stable after work at different hours of the day. I noticed that his legs became swollen after he had worked. When this happens after some days of rest during which the horse is not moved, it is a sign of bad digestion. But, immediately after work, this swelling indicates heart trouble. We asked a professor veterinarian to examine his heart, and he found that a muscle of the heart and the valves were wrecked. There were days when the horse felt fright because the heart did not work regularly, and the more he was forced to go, the more fright he showed. This horse was useless as a performer for modern sport. At any moment he might have a heart attack even at the walk. We had to get rid of him.

In our team we used to take the temperatures of the horses every day. The horse is not able to tell us that he feels badly. Perhaps he has a headache, or some other trouble. We take the horse to his daily work and sometimes we do not realize that he is ill, which is why he is not willing to work as he usually does. We take our car to be checked over at frequent intervals. We rarely bother to do the same with our horses. The better we know our horse and the more care we give him, the longer he will perform well for our pleasure and satisfaction.

2.
Gaits of the Horse

THE NATURAL GAITS OF THE HORSE

Generally speaking the average well bred and normally
built horse uses four gaits to move his body from one place
to another. They are—

Walk

Trot—extended, ordinary, or slow

Canter and gallop—which is the easiest way for him to
cover ground quickly. Gallop can
be ordinary, fast.

The Walk

The walk is perhaps the most complicated of all the
horse's movements. We hear four beats: pa-ta-pa-ta, pa-ta-
pa-ta, pa-ta-pa-ta. . . . When the horse is walking correctly
on pavement, we hear four beats at equal intervals and of
equal sound; when the horse is sore on one leg, he puts it on
the ground a little more gently and we can hear distinctly
that one beat is not as strong as the others. When we start
counting the beats, for example, from the (near) *left* front
leg, then the next leg which touches the ground will be the

47

(off) *right* hind, then comes the right front, and then the left hind: Left—right,—left—right. When we start counting from the near *left* hind leg, then the sequence is: near left front, off right hind, then off right front. Near left— near left,—off right—off right. The walk is a gait which has no moment of suspension, that means the horse is all the time touching the ground, he is never in the air. His body is supported by three legs, or two diagonal, or two lateral legs.[x]

As you can see, the horse has to move his balance or his point of gravity from one side to the other and forward. Naturally he must help this action by moving his neck accordingly. That is why at the walk, particularly an extended walk, the horse's neck moves up and down and forward, and his back also works in a very distinct way. The horse, disturbed by the rider's hands and body, cannot use himself freely, and he either slows his walk or starts to "jig." Some horses, when disturbed by the rider so that they can't use their neck correctly, develop a fast irregular walk which can change into the pace.

Pacing: In olden times when the rider did not know the benefit of posting,[1] the sitting trot was constantly used. This was uncomfortable for the rider and tiring for the horse. People therefore appreciated a horse who moved at the *pace*. One even made special efforts to train horses to pace —a gait which is smoother for the non-posting rider and faster than the walk. Generally speaking, the pace is the natural gait of a camel, not a horse. However, a horse who

---

[x] Remark: By diagonal we understand two legs touching the ground at the same time: left diagonal being left (near) front (off) hind leg. The right diagonal is vice versa.
By lateral we understand two legs on the same side of the horse's body stepping on the ground at the same time.

[1] See Part II, Chapter 7.

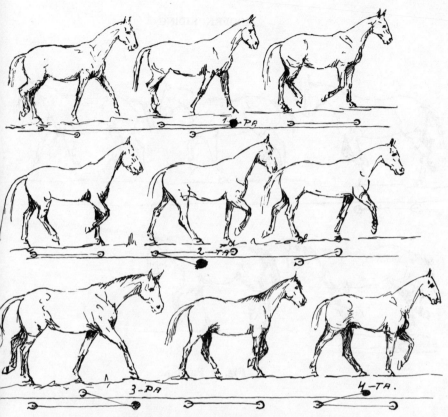

Fig. 5 Walk. Illustrating the sequence of movement of the horse's legs and the way they support his body.

is not allowed to use himself naturally at the walk, falls into the camel habit of pacing. If this habit is firmly established, it is very difficult to retrain the horse to walk correctly.

When the extended walk is correct, the marks on the ground made by the hind legs over-reach the marks of the front legs. In the ordinary walk, the hind legs step exactly into the marks of the front legs. In the slow walk, which we don't use, and which the dressage school calls the collected

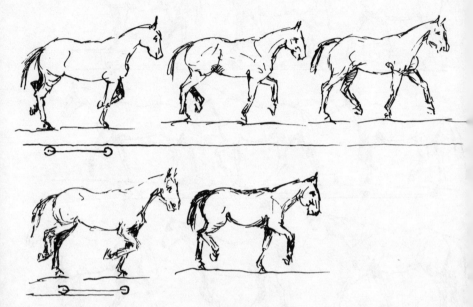

Fig. 6 Pacing.

walk, the horse does not reach with the hind legs the marks of the front legs.

The Trot

If you observe the horse in a state of freedom in the field, you will notice that he does not use the trot very much. He walks and gallops. He uses the trot as sort of a temporary transition between walking and galloping. Sometimes when he plays, he shows himself in an extended trot, which is a most spectacular movement. Sometimes, when very excited, he even shows in "passage," which is a trot of very great impulsion but of high movement, more up than forward.

This sort of trot (passage) belongs to the movements of high school and we will leave it to the dressage riders to use when they train for the high school.

We will deal only with the normal trot: ordinary, slow, and extended. The latter (one) is a physical exercise for the impulse forward, stretching the joints and muscles, etc. This trot is very tiring for the horse when executed for too long a time or distance. (Bad riders who do not understand the horse, when going for a hack[1] oftentimes use the extended trot most of the time. This is very bad. It excites the horse and makes him tired. One should walk fast and freely, and trot at a moderate speed, rather slow than too fast, and gallop freely, which the horse likes best.) The trot is the least complicated movement of all the horse's gaits. We hear two beats —hop—hop,—hop—hop, hop—hop, hop —hop, at equal intervals, and with equal sound. The horse in forward movement pushes his body using the hind legs, which take a slightly larger step than the front legs are capable of doing. The front legs have to make a step equal to that of the hind legs, which is why they must hop forward. Here comes the moment of suspension. The horse starts to jump from one diagonal to the other. Why diagonal? Because the diagonal legs touching the ground can support and balance the horse's body in a straight line. The rider can feel the up and down but not the movement sideways. The neck of the horse does not make any visible movement, just slightly in the area of the withers; the head of the horse does not move. The trot is executed by the legs and the back muscles which always work more during the moment of suspension.

[1] hack—pleasure riding in the country, usually without jumping. (French—promenade)

1. Hop!

TROT.

2- Hop!

Fig. 7 Trot.

Canter and Gallop

I believe that man was not far from the monkey in his development when he decided to tame the horse and ride on his back; he wanted to be faster than he could be on his own two clumsy legs. So he tamed the horse and galloped cross country to hunt animals or to fight his enemies who were on foot. I imagine that when the first riders appeared and attacked other people who were on foot, they made an even greater impression than the explosion of the first atomic bomb in Hiroshima in our modern time. The panic I imagine was so great that people created a legend about some monsters: half horse, half man, which we know from mythological times as centaurs. Since the time of those mythological creatures until our modern times, through thousands and thousands of years, the greatest pleasure for a horseman and his horse was, and will be, to gallop across rough country. The rhythm of a gallop, for us, has something of music. The horse used the gallop mostly in freedom when travelling from one place to another looking for better food or water. The horse enjoys gallop or canter most, because it is a gait which enables him to make bigger strides with less effort.

At the *canter,* which is a gallop of moderate speed, the horse throws his body, like a spear, from behind to the front. He gives a sort of elevation for his back; the front legs at this moment leave the ground; the horse is in the air, in suspension, to give time and opportunity for the hind legs (the pushing motor) to come under the body and give a push. The front legs support the body, and in co-ordination with the movement of the neck, they leave the ground and again give the elevation for the horse's body which is at this moment again in suspension, and so on—the push from behind is repeated. We hear three beats in the canter—

pa-ta-*pam,* pa-ta-*pam,* pa-ta-*pam.* I stress the "pam," the third beat, to show that when cantering correctly the horse accentuates the last beat. After this "pam" comes the moment of suspension. The horse is in the air, to touch the ground again with his hind legs.

When we hear sort of pa-ra-ta-pam, pa-ra-ta-pam, where the "ta" is stronger than the "pam," it shows that the horse is losing his impetus. There is no moment of suspension; the horse does not canter, he crawls. He has lost the forward impulse and canters much too slowly. We could compare it with driving a car with a standard gear shift. When you come, for example, to a speed below 20 miles per hour you must change into second gear, otherwise the engine does not work rhythmically. The horse canters leading with his left front leg, or leading with his right front leg, stretching left diagonal or right diagonal. When he starts to gallop with the leading right leg, he puts the left hind leg on the ground first and gives the push to the body; this would be the first beat—"pa"; next comes the diagonal: right hind and left front leg—"ta" together as one beat, and then comes "pam" the beat of the right front leg. Then comes the moment of suspension. The horse is in the air and again puts his left hind leg on the ground.

If he decides to change the direction and to change the leg leading, he does it in that moment—during the suspension. Instead of putting the *left* hind leg on the ground normally, he puts the right hind leg, and then the diagonal —*left* hind and *right* front, and finally the *left* front leg.

At the canter the horse uses his neck to help himself in getting into the moment of suspension and uses the muscles of his back to give the elevation to the body and to transmit the push from behind to the front.

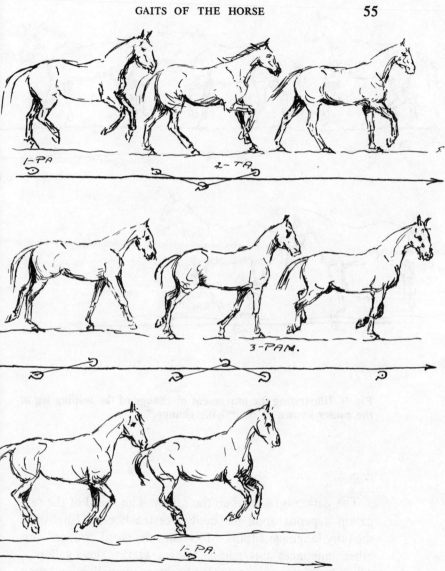

Fig. 8 Canter.

Fig. 9 Illustrating the movement of change of the leading leg at the canter known as the "flying change."

Gallop

The gallop is faster than the canter. The speed of the fast gallop depends upon the quality of the horse. (English is the only language I think which uses the word "canter"—in other languages this gait is known as the slow gallop—which as the speed is increased becomes the gallop, and then the fast gallop.) To gallop fast, the horse must give a much bigger push with his hind legs than is required to canter. He

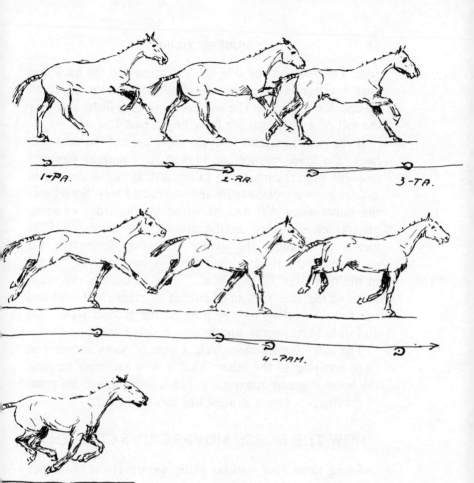

Fig. 10 Gallop.

pushes, first with the one hind leg and then the other, depending on the leading leg. He throws his body rapidly forward supporting it by stretching out his front legs, according to the speed. He uses his front legs separately, one after the other, making as big a step as the push from behind demands.. He therefore divides the diagonal and we hear four beats, the last being the strongest—pa-ra-ta-*pam,* pa-ra-ta-

pam. The neck on one side of the withers and the back and hind quarters on the other co-ordinate the movement, in an up and down motion. The withers move very little, and play the roll of a pivot, simply travelling forward.

If the rider interferes with the movement of the neck and back, the horse cannot use himself in a normal way and loses his natural capacity to gallop fast. He slows down and gallops in an uncomfortable and contracted way. Sometimes the horse when disbalanced either by the rider or some unexpected difficulty on the ground gets *disunited*. This means he changes the canter or gallop from left, for example, to the right in the front legs but does not change in the hind legs, or vice versa. Then he canters this way: *left* hind leg, then instead of putting together *right* hind and *left* front legs diagonal, he puts on the ground *right* hind and *right* front lateral, and finally the left front.

The rider immediately feels a sort of jerky movement, from one side to the other. This is very incorrect because the horse is going unnaturally. He is disbalanced; his point of gravity is not on a straight line but in zig zag.

HOW THE HORSE MOVES CROSS COUNTRY

Using these four natural gaits, we travel on horseback across country which sometimes can be very hilly and rough. To know how to facilitate the horse's work under our weight, we must know how the horse uses himself naturally, when negotiating the various obstacles he may meet. We may be confronted by a variety of difficulties, such as ditches, vertical fences, on flat ground or where there is a different level between take-off and landing point. We may find banks, ploughed fields, and water, or hills that are so steep that to pass down them the horse must slide in a manner resembling a modern skier.

Miss Margee Andison on "Sandy," during a lesson in Winnipeg, after one week of training. Notice the correct position of the leg and lightness of the hand.

(Photo—Miss E. Geiger)

At Jumps

When approaching an obstacle, the horse pays attention from afar and tries to judge the size and proportions of the fence. If he thinks it is possible for him to negotiate the obstacle successfully, and be on the other side, he prepares himself for the jump. He judges the distance and as he approaches, gathers the necessary energy and momentum. He watches carefully for the best point for his take-off. If the horse takes off too far back, he must give his body a bigger push. When confronted by a simple straight fence, this is not so important. However, a great deal of trouble can be caused by a "too-soon take-off" when negotiating a larger obstacle, such as spread fence or a wide ditch on the other side of the fence. If the horse takes off too late, he could easily hit it with his front legs. If the fence is straight, he might clear it without accident; however, he could eventually disbalance himself and stumble. But if there is a ditch behind a straight fence, or the ground on the landing side is lower than the side of the take-off, and the take-off is too late, disaster could follow.

Some horses have the natural instinct of approach. They always do it correctly. I should say that most horses, when jumping without a rider and of their own free will, hardly ever make a mistake in judging the distance to the fence.

The actual jump then follows. The horse in his last stride of gallop lowers his hind quarters and bends his hind legs putting them under his body. The neck stretches towards the obstacle, helping the front legs to leave the ground at the same time. The horse lifts his withers according to the elevation of the fence. Now the hind legs straighten themselves and give the necessary push. The horse's body is thrown in the air following the arc as described by the withers. The front legs should be folded as much as possible,

Miss S. Lewis from the U.S.A. during the lesson in Brussels. Very good harmony in movement over triple barre, 7′ spread and 4′ high. The head of the rider could be higher. Notice the position of the leg.

(Photo—A. Dobrski, Brussels)

so that the body will not travel too high. The neck performs tremendous work. First it stretches to the fence for the take off and then lowers slightly. Then the horse uses his neck muscles to help take his front legs off the ground. He lowers it again and stretches it down following the direction of an arc, helping the body, particularly the hind quarters, to get over the fence more easily. Gradually, as the hind legs start to fold, the front legs stretch in preparation to land. As soon as the hind legs are over the fence, the neck resumes its normal position, helping the horse establish his balance on the ground. Both front legs do not touch the ground together. The leading leg of the canter which the horse used when approaching the fence touches the ground first. If the horse made his approach with the right leg leading, the right leg is first on the ground, followed by the left front leg which takes a step forward, to give sufficient space for the hindquarters. This step forward amortizes the shock the horse would otherwise receive, which is up to ten times the weight of his body. Then again the neck helps the front to leave the ground and permits the hind legs to touch the ground. Between the landing moment of the front legs and the landing moment of the hind legs, there is a moment of suspension, because the horse maintains his gallop. During this instant the horse usually changes the lead. He does it at the moment when he makes a step with the front legs after landing with the leading leg. For example: The horse approaches a fence at a canter leading with his right leg. When he lands, he puts the leading leg on the ground first, in this case the right leg. He then steps forward with the left leg. At this moment of being in the air the hind legs adjust themselves to land. This is done in relation to the position of the front legs. As now the left front leg is leading, the right hind leg lands first, and immediately after the left hind leg. The horse continues his canter, but he has changed the lead. The horse behaves this way when jumping undisturbed over a fence. When the horse decides to turn to the right or to the left after the jump, he changes his lead either in the next stride or has already done so in the air. He then lands, according to his intention, on the right or on the left leg, depending on which direction he will turn.

When jumping ditches, the horse works basically the same way as when approaching straight fences. From afar he judges the size and proportions of the ditch. He then decides to gallop over it. When the edge of the ditch is open and clearly marked, the horse approaches at a gallop, increasing his pace to give greater impulsion. He selects the point of take-off as close as possible to the ditch and behaves more or less in the same way as in a normal jump. When the edge of the ditch is not clearly defined and the horse is unable to judge the size and has difficulty in picking his take-off point, he slows his pace, very often up to a standstill. He examines the ditch quickly, coming as close as possible to the edge, lowering his neck. Then with his hind legs under his body, he gathers all his energy and throws himself from a standstill over the ditch, catching the other edge with his front legs. Then the neck stretches with great strength and rapidity down and forward to enable the hind legs to come quickly under his body, catching the ground just behind the front legs. The tremendous work of the neck at this moment permits the horse to continue his movement forward on the other side of the ditch.

In County Meath in Ireland when you follow the Word Union hounds, you very often come upon ditches which are very big and deep. They are often times more than twelve or thirteen feet wide and up to eight feet deep, and one is unable to see the actual edge of the ditch from afar, due to undergrowth and a tangle of weeds. I presume the reason why the ditches are so deep is because the Irish farmers have been digging them deeper ever since the time of St. Patrick, and so the only safe way for a horse to travel over them is to stop, have a look, and then jump from a standstill.

When going over rough, deep, soft ground such as a heavy wet ploughed field, or a bog, the horse's hind quarters work very much harder than when the going is easy. He lowers his head and neck. His back muscles are also more engaged. He puts his legs onto the ground very carefully and pulls them out slowly, instinctively endeavoring to avoid sinking too deeply into the mud or bog. The neck at this time plays the role of the balancing factor, similar to the hands of a human being in a similar situation.

Slopes

When going downhill, the horse uses his hind legs as brakes. The steeper the slope, the smaller steps the horse takes at the walk. His hind legs come under his body, which is inclined downwards in relation to the slope of the hill. To facilitate the hard work of the hind legs, the horse puts as much weight as possible on the front legs, which play the role of supporting crutches even more then when on flat ground. The neck lowers and stretches. The horse does not like to trot downhill; he prefers to either walk slowly or to canter. At this time his cantering is done with small downward hops (jumps). The hind legs do not push, they brake, which is why they touch the ground almost simultaneously. The front legs moving carefully do the same. The neck, stretched, moves up and down, particularly the part of the neck nearest the withers. The back muscles work like ropes, holding the body in the proper inclination.

Steep Slides

There are places in rough country where the ground suddenly drops away, forming an almost perpendicular wall. It is surprising how the horse can slide down a precipice up to 75°, once he has learned to use himself. Difficult slides are less dangerous than the deep ditches of Ireland because when maneuvering them, he cannot fall upside down or somersault; rather he falls sideways due to the fact that his hind legs have slipped. This is the reason why the horse should always go straight down, never at an angle. The hind legs are drawn well under the body and stretched, so that the hocks do not touch the ground. The front legs are straight and stretched forward. The neck and head are stretched and free to keep the horse balanced.

The ground is so steep that the horse cannot move a step forward. By putting his legs and body in the position described above, and using his legs like skis, he slides down to a point three or four feet from the bottom. He then jumps on to the level ground. While sliding, the body of the horse only moves forward, it does not change its position.

Uphill

It is interesting to observe a horse going uphill. He uses himself instinctively in relation to the inclination of the hill. When the hill is long and not too steep, he walks, using his hind legs as a motor, pushing him forward. Again the neck stretches forward and down, using a jerky motion at every step, thus facilitating the work of the hind legs.

If the hill is long and the ground soft but *not* slippery, he goes on a zig zag pattern, thus making his ascent easier.

If the slope is short and steep, he gives his body impulse and gallops up. This speed uses his muscles less, and the heart and lungs more.

Observing and studying the free movements of the horse, we conclude that if we want to have a good performer for cross country riding, a safe, comfortable animal, able to cope with any difficulty—

(a) he must be well shaped
(b) he must move correctly
(c) he must have good legs, a good shoulder, a strong back, a proportionately long neck, and a good character. His character will be good if all his senses are normal, and he has been well treated, and carefully and thoughtfully trained.

3.

The Mentality of the Horse

As we mentioned before, modern riding consists of co-operation between the horse and rider, *based on confidence in each other*. To build up this confidence, the rider should try to understand not only the horse's physical structure and his natural movements, but also his mentality and his mental reaction to the different impressions and experiences he meets during his life with the rider.

Most of the great masters of equitation consider the horse as an animal without any intelligence. I think that what we *understand* as intelligence, the horse has in very limited form. Anyhow, much less than, for example, the dog. Perhaps this is because the horse of today generally works only one or two hours with people and then stands alone in the stable, very often with his head against the wall, and has no diversion.

The horses of the Arabs, or the Kirges in South Siberia, who live together with humans almost from the time they

66

are born, are more clever than our horses. During my life-time, I have seen horses which showed some intelligence, though limited. For example, in 1929 I travelled with four-teen horses of our jumping team through Germany, France, and then to Nice for the international show jumping. The horses travelled in three carriages. In each carriage, as well as the horses, there was plenty of forage, trunks and the personal belongings of the riders and grooms. The trunks were placed in front of the horses so that they could be used as small platforms for the feeding buckets. We travelled six days, changing trains many times. In Germany, when our cars were detached from one train and pushed to another, it was done very gently. The animals were not disturbed in any way. But when we passed the French frontier in Stras-bourg, the employees of the French railways behaved as if there were stones rather than animals in our carriage. Again we changed trains frequently, and each time before the engine was attached to move us to another train, there was a sharp whistle, followed immediately by a terrific bump or jerk. The horses fell with their knees against the trunks, oftentimes hurting themselves, or as we moved for-ward they fell back and bumped their hindquarters against the wall behind them. Naturally they were frightened and excited. After two days we arrived at Lyon, a large junction. We had breakfast, fed the horses and were ready to be attached to the fast train to go to Marseilles. Before we moved, my corporal veterinarian, who traveled in another carriage, came to me and asked me, "Will you come to my carriage and look at something which is curious?" I went. Soon we heard a sharp whistle. At the same moment the horses pricked their ears, showing great excitement, except one whose name was "Matador," an Irish horse. He quietly put one front leg on top of the trunk and pushed his hind-quarter against the wall. He fixed himself in this way and waited for the bump or jerk which came inevitably. The other horses were knocked about and were very annoyed. "Matador" took it calmly. He had fixed himself in a stationary position by using his own ingenuity. When the train moved ahead, he took his leg off the trunk and started to eat his hay as though nothing had happened. Through his intelligence he had worked out a way to avoid the unpleasant jerks and bumps. I had a horse who switched on the electricity by turning the knob in his box. He did it only when he became annoyed while waiting for his food, to show the groom who fed the other horses that he was there and waiting for his dinner.

Memory

No doubt the horse has an extraordinary *memory*. He remembers forever some things which particularly frightened him or were very unpleasant. That is why one should start the training of your animals very carefully, avoiding any battles or unpleasant moments. Of course, the horse also remembers the pleasures and the circumstances under which pleasant things happened very well.

The horse receives all the impressions, and reacts to them by using his senses. The senses are like those of a human being—sight, hearing, smell, taste, and touch.

Sight

The horse's eyes are placed on either side of his forehead, which is why he has a wider field of vision than does the human. The slightest turn of his head allows him to see what is going on behind him. In the night he sees much better than we do. The eyes of the horse are phosphorescent in the night as are the eyes of a cat.

No doubt he distinguishes colors. Some horses are Daltonists—to them everything seems grey. I have seen horses that hated the color white. There are horses that have astigmatism or ametropia of the lens, and to them everything appears blurred or distorted. They shy and show some excitement when meeting some objects which they are unable to identify. Naturally one should not force the horse in that case by using a whip or spurs. The rider should behave rather indifferently, convincing the horse by his calmness that there is no need to be frightened.

I took part in international show jumping in Rome in 1931. There were over 200 horses competing. Naturally the competition was going on non-stop until late in the evening. In order to write the marks, the "jury" had to use torches. The lights were on in Villa Borghese and on the streets of the city. In spite of the fact that I jumped at a fast speed and did not see some rustic fences, the horse jumped better and with greater care than in daylight. I completed the parcours without fault.

Once during maneuvers, after a party where we had too many drinks, four Lieutenants, coming back to our quarters, decided to gallop cross country, which was unknown territory to us. We jumped ditches and barbed wire fences without any trouble. It was late at night and although there was a lovely moon, we did not see the fences. However, the horses did. I believe God must take into his care the fools and the drunk people. At that time we probably received double care as we arrived home without a scratch.

Hearing

Hearing is perhaps the most developed of the horse's senses. The ears, like radar instruments, turn in all directions, catching every noise from very far. Very sensitive horses show some excitement on hearing noises they probably cannot understand. The rider very often does not understand the reason for excitement because he does not hear the noise which the horse's ear has picked up. The horse is sensitive to a voice, but he doesn't understand the words. For example, we can use very rude words but in a sweet caressing voice, and they please the horse. We can use the most wonderful pet words, but if shouted in an angry voice, we can frighten the horse. I have never met a horse that would march in rhythm to music. If you see a horse in a circus trotting or galloping, or doing a Spanish Walk in time to music, it is the orchestra leader who conducts the music in accordance with the horse's movements. However, horses can remember, for example, trumpet signals with which they associate some function, such as food, trot, gallop.

There is a very well known story about one old cavalry horse who was sold to a farmer. The farmer was harrowing his field, and suddenly from behind a hill where some cavalry were having exercises, one could hear a trumpet sounding the signal for roll-call. Before the farmer could understand what was happening, the horse ran away, dragging the harrow behind him. He joined the squadron, placing himself obediently on the left flank of the squadron as he had done so many times in his life.

Smell

This sense is also very well developed in the horse. He likes pleasant odors and hates bad smells. (Of course, what is bad for us might not be bad for a horse.) Many horses simply cannot stand the smell of pigs. I had a young Anglo-Arab who suddenly stopped dead while traveling across country, and I could not persuade him to go forward at all. I had no idea why. After a long time of persuasion, I noticed that there was a farm with many pigs a quarter of a mile away. I had to repeat the struggle every time I passed this farm.

In the cavalry we had to train squadrons quickly and efficiently to go into the transport train. Of course one had to train the horses to get used to the train and to go obediently in and out of the carriage. One young horse did not want to go in. The lancers tried to force him by using a rope behind his legs. I came along and stopped this. I petted the horse, and I took a handkerchief which a lady had given me, it had a lovely smell—Houbigant or Chanel No. 5. I let the horse smell it and he suddenly followed me without any trouble into the carriage. This particular horse probably was very sensitive to "French Perfume," like his Squadron leader. This does not mean that every horse would do the same thing, but it shows that horses, like men, are sensitive and susceptible!

Touch

If a horse approaching a fence at a walk stretches his neck and head, and touches it with his nose, it does not necessarily mean that he smells the fence. This is rather connected with his sense of touch. He examines the fence by touching it with the hair on his lips, which is very sensitive.

You might notice some time, when approaching a pole lying on the ground, that a young horse touches it with his hoof. The hooves, particularly the tips of the front hooves, are also very sensitive. (I will mention it further when describing the training of a jumper over cavaletti.)

The whole body of the horse—his mouth, his skin, and so on, has nerves which make him sensitive to touch. Some horses, like people, are born more sensitive than others.

At one time I trained a young Anglo-Arab, a strong animal with good bones, about sixteen hands. I started to lunge[1] him. He trotted well for a while, but after about five

[1] Exercise on the lunging rein—See Part III, Chapter 1.

minutes he stopped. I tried to convince him to trot on, moving the whip behind him, but to no avail. I whipped him. He looked at me as if I were not there and did not move. I dropped the lunge on the ground, and I went behind him and whipped him several times, as hard as I could just to make him go—it did not matter how. Believe it or not, the horse did not move. I whipped him like old trousers and I still made no impression. His sensitivity was somehow underdeveloped. Later on, after much training, he turned out to be a very good hunter and officer's charger, but it took a long time and a great deal of patience to develop his reaction to my legs and hands.

The horse's sense of touch is probably the most important thing to be taken into consideration during training. The more sensitive the horse is, the more carefully he must be handled by the trainer. We must remember that it is always better to invite the horse to be obedient than to force him. Of course, one has to treat every horse individually. One horse has to be handled very gently and very gradually in order to diminish his sensitivity, and another has to be treated quite roughly until he becomes more sensitive and obedient.

From my long experience, I prefer the sensitive horse, rather than one who is sluggish and common. The fastest and best results are obtained with sensitive horses.

Taste

Horses like sugar and salt, and they are able to distinguish other tastes. We very often give carrots or sugar to a horse as a reward when he has understood us and executed our order willingly. But personally, I do not suggest giving sugar too often. Some ladies like to come to the stable and give sugar to their "pet" without any reason. As a result the horse loses his good manners and begins to behave like a spoiled child who bothers his mother, always asking for some sweets. I have seen many horses which were quite annoyed with me when I did not give them sugar. One even turned his hindquarters towards me and intended to kick me, he was so cross that he did not get sugar. The best "sugar" is to treat the horse in a sweet way when riding him.

Some riders who give sugar in the stable, later put on a standing martingale,[1] dropped noseband,[2] and twisted snaffle, gag[3] or some other "start" machinery in the mouth and annoy the horse, jerking his mouth, bumping on his back and simply murdering him. So let us give sugar or carrots during work as a reward, but not in the stable. Horses will have much better manners if they are petted by their owners and *rewarded* at the right moment in the proper way. Horses like to be scratched on the withers, under the lower lip, and so on. We can play with the horse as much as we like, and this makes him kinder and more polite. His confidence in us grows, but we must never spoil him.

Instincts

We mention that a well trained horse should not lose his temper and stability when finding himself in a dangerous situation. We can achieve this only by respecting and properly exploiting the natural instincts of the horse during the time of training. This applies mostly to jumpers and cross country horses.

First of all the horse has an extremely well-developed instinct of self-preservation, and we should take this instinct

---

[1] standing martingale—a strong strap attached to the noseband, goes between front legs, under the chest and attached to the girth.

[2] dropped noseband—noseband under the bit. Prevents opening the horse's mouth.

[3] gag—specially constructed bridge. Pulls on the mouth and at the same time presses in the spot where the head is connected to the neck.

under consideration. We should let the horse use it to the
benefit of both himself and his rider.

As an example: We may gallop across unknown rough
country and arrive at a very steep slope. Of course a horse,
undisturbed by the rider, coming to this dangerous place,
will slow down and look carefully to see where to put his
legs and how to use himself so that he will make the descent
without an accident. This will be the moment of subcon-
sciously using his own instinct of self-preservation. Undisturbed and undeterred by the rider, the horse will behave
properly. However, if the rider tries to dictate what to do,
the horse becomes frightened by this interference, will lose
his temper, and instead of using his instinct, will try to take
some desperate action to liberate himself from any interference. Very often the results will be catastrophic.

A. The horse disturbed by the rider jumps down the
   slope.
B. The horse behaves correctly because the rider lets
   him use the neck freely.

Or, another example: We approach a fence. Instead of
letting the horse judge the distance and pick out the best
point at which to take off, the rider starts to judge the distance himself. Naturally the horse does not want to have an
accident. Instinctively he will approach the fence in the
proper way to find the right place for taking off, and will
use himself in a natural way to negotiate the jump without
mistake. But when the rider starts to interfere and starts to
judge the distance and "time" the horse, the animal loses
his temper and gets excited, rushes to the fence, and thinks
more about how to get rid of the "help" of the rider than
how to negotiate the jump. That is why we see so many so-
called "open jumpers" exploding over fences. Everything
is all right when the rider has great experience in this

Fig. 11 (A) Copy of a photo of an Italian officer on a slide before Caprilli and (B) the descent of a horse according to Caprilli.

"judging of distance," but if the rider makes a mistake, then comes disaster. A very ambitious and generous horse does his best to avoid accidents, and this is why he explodes over fences, using twice as much energy as should be necessary in normal conditions. Correct *co-operation between horse and rider* is therefore essential. The rider gives the order, which the horse executes.

The horse is naturally *gregarious*. In his natural state, he lived in a community. The leader of the "clan" was responsible for order, security, food, and water, etc. As a result, horses instinctively like to be in the company of other horses or other live creatures like donkeys, dogs, and human beings. It is much easier to train a young horse in the company of an old, well-trained sensible animal. The youngster will follow the good example, for horses are mimics.

I remember in our jumping team we had a horse called "Zaratusta." He was small, 15.2 hands, black, a very strong Anglo-Arab with the face of a philosopher, a clever and very promising jumper. The boxes in our stable were built in such a way that the bigger horses could look out, stretching their necks so that they could see what was going on in the stable. They could have some amusement. But poor Zaratusta was too small to look out of the box. He was miserable. He could not see what was going on in the corridor, and he was naturally inquisitive. Of course he was also unable to communicate with his neighbors. He walked around and around his big box, stretching his neck and head as much as he could, endeavoring to see over the partition. It was useless. The wooden partition between the box and the corridor of the stable was much too high for him. Suddenly, one day he had an idea. Inside the box there was a beam about two feet above the ground level. This was part of the construction of the box. He used this. He put his front legs on the beam, and to his astonishment he could see more than even the large horses. He stuck his neck out like a giraffe, and stood that way practically all the time between his meals. After a week or more we had many giraffes in our stable. The other big horses started to imitate little Zaratusta, and four or five of them used the same trick as he did to look out of their boxes. It was simple and they found that they could have much more amusement.

Horses trained in a group usually make better progress than those trained alone. But we must not forget that exaggeration is not good. The well trained horse should be obedient when alone and in company. He should not be distracted by the presence or absence of other animals. That is why we should sometimes train the horse alone, and sometimes in the company of other horses.

The horse should be accustomed to his rider and should enjoy his company. Of course, this is possible only when the rider behaves like a companion to his horse.

Food

Partly dictated by self-preservation there is another instinct—the instinct for food. The horse likes to go to the stable as he knows that he gets food there. Horses which are kept in an outside paddock do not bother as much about the stable. However, the horses that are kept in a stable most of the time are drawn to the stable; they are most anxious to return to their box. This can be used as a help during their training.

For example: We train a young horse in a paddock or covered arena, and we practice striking into a canter on the correct lead. The gate is C. The horse most of the time is thinking about the gate, and how to get out to the stable

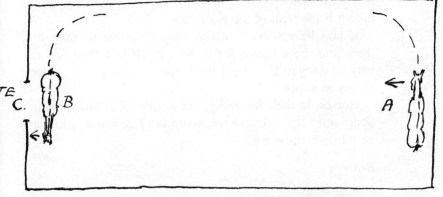

Fig. 12 The arrows show the direction of distraction of the horse.

where he can get food and rest. As a result, all his attention is directed to the gate. When we work to the left and we ask the horse to start the canter to the left, it is much easier to do it in position "A" than in position "B," because the mentality of the horse and also physical attitude is in the direction of the gate. So when we ask the horse to canter in position "A," the horse does it easily. When we ask him to do it in position "B," all his attention is to the right and he will ignore our indication to canter left. In spite of our correct indication he will canter on the opposite leg, because all he wants is to reach the gate which is on the right side. This natural tendency of the horse should be taken into consideration.

When we follow this instinct of the horse logically, we get much quicker and better results without any battle.

One could write volumes about the mentality of the horse, and other volumes about co-operation between the two mentalities of the horse and rider. To make a long story short: when you have some difficulty, some misunderstanding between you and your horse, *before acting try to find the reason why*. And believe it or not, 99 per cent of the time it is the fault of the rider.

If you have a horse which causes trouble or difficulty, there must be a reason for it. First of all you must find out why he does it. If you get the correct diagnosis the remedy is easy to apply.

Horses, in their mentality, are a little like human beings. Some are very co-operative, some are suspicious, some are very brave, some not.

Bravery

And what is bravery?

I think that, for example, a brave man is not a man who does not realize the danger. He is a man who feels the dan-

ger. He is frightened, but by his will he supresses the fright
and does what he has to do. This is the brave man, and not
the man who does something brave because of ignorance.

Horses are the same. Some are brave because they face a
dangerous situation calmly and do what they should. Some
become confused and refuse to face the danger.

Then in riding comes the moment of co-operation
between the rider and the horse. When the horse loses his
courage, the rider should encourage him by his determination and will. There is a well known saying, "Throw your
heart over the fence and the horse will follow it." The horse,
like a barometer, has the ability to feel the disposition and
spirit of the rider.

One rider will jump his horse over fences, and the same
horse with another rider will refuse even the smallest jump.
Why? Because the first rider gave the order distinctly and
was determined to force his horse if perchance the horse
hesitated. The other rider was not sure of himself, his order
was not clear; also there was no determination.

Fright

Very often a young horse shows excitement and fright
because he meets something which is new to him. If the
rider gives him confidence in a calm way, the horse becomes
confident.

For example, police horses ignore traffic, shouting of
crowds, and so on, because they are trained very gradually
and thoroughly, and become accustomed to all sorts of
experiences they may encounter during their duty. Likewise,
in the army, horses are trained to ignore all explosions,
shooting, and movements of swords and lances, which
frightened them at the beginning of their military career.

After the First World War we had a chief instructor, an
extraordinary rider, particularly in cross country, Colonel

Adamowic from the Austrian cavalry. He told us a very interesting story. He belonged to the life guard squadron of the Emperor of Austria, Franz Josef II. One of the officers had a mare, which was absolutely impossible in front of the platoon. She was very nervous, always excited, frightened of everything that was going on around her during duty. The Commanding Officer of the life guard was so annoyed that he forbade this officer to appear on his mare in front of the platoon—and the mare was an exceptionally good looking animal. The owner decided to sell her, and so one day the "schtalmaster of the Emperor" arrived at the barracks, and asked to see the mare. He liked her and decided to buy her for the Kaiser, Franz Josef II, and Franz Josef was nortorious for being very particular about horses. (Once he had a marvellous horse from Ireland which he rode in the Prater. Suddenly a tiny dog jumped out of the bushes and barking, attacked the horse. The horse got frightened and balked. The Kaiser never mounted this horse again.)

When the "schtalmaster" decided to buy this mare, the officers told him that she was absolutely unsuitable for the Kaiser, and explained how badly she behaved and what a bad temperament she had. "Never mind," said the schtalmaster. "I will take her." One year later one could see Franz Josef II riding the mare on the Prater, the mare behaving like an angel.

"What did you do to her?" asked the officer of the schtalmaster. "She is a difficult animal."

The schtalmaster explained that he rode the mare in the manege, where he brought in boys from the street to make as much noise and trouble as possible. They shouted, they played football or other games, they ran, they fought, they made shooting noises, and did all sorts of things which would make it more confusing and noisy for the mare. This happened every day. After two or three months the mare became accustomed to these circumstances, becoming a little quieter, and gradually ignored them. Then he rode her in the Prater. When the mare found herself in circumstances much more pleasant and quieter than the manege, she became as quiet as a lamb.

One cannot say that a born coward can be transformed into a hero, but by correct education and patience, extraordinary results can be achieved.

PART II.
THE RIDER

1.
The Rider

James Fillis, the famous circus rider at the end of the 19th century, who was appointed as chief instructor in the Russian Cavalry School, says in one of his books that when the training of a horse is accomplished only one brain works—the brain of the rider. In other words, the horse stops thinking for himself and begins to work like an automaton. The rider decides everything, even which leg the horse uses and how he should put it on the ground. But natural equitation does not deprive the horse of his own initiative. The horse uses his brain, his instincts, and his natural abilities while listening to the orders of his rider. Here the rider gives the order and as soon as the horse has understood and is prepared to execute it, the rider lets him do so, helping him by adapting himself to the horse's movement. The rider is passive, but ready to correct the horse if he feels that the horse does something not quite in the line with the rider's intention. This is the difference between the old school and the new "natural equitation."

How the rider communicates his will to the horse

The good rider gives the orders to the horse in a very simple way and at the right moment. First, he calls the horse to attention and then gives the order. *Never take the horse by surprise.* All movements *forward,* the rider orders *using his legs.* All movements *back,* such as decreasing the pace, changing from gallop to trot or walk, halting, reining back—the rider orders by *using his hands.* Changing the direction to the right or left, the rider gives his orders using the right hand or the left. *The hands and the legs never act at the same time.*

When the hands act—the legs are passive.

When the legs act—the hands are passive.

Hands—Contact

To call the horse to attention and be ready to give the order, the rider must first connect himself with the horse. He takes the reins and attaches his hands to the horse's mouth in such a way, that from the horse's mouth to the rider's elbows, the hands with the reins form a straight line. Why a straight line? Because the shortest distance between two points is the straight line, and the action of the elbow gives the strongest and quickest result. The pulling is softer when in a straight line. A broken line between snaffle and elbow results in a stiffened wrist. When you pull, the wrist should be relaxed, i.e., straight. The arms from the shoulders to the elbows are hanging freely, relaxed —*never stuck to the body.* The hands are holding the reins between the small finger and the third, and between the thumb and the first finger. *All fingers are rounded and never closed;* the wrist straight, soft, and relaxed. The part of the arm between the wrist and elbow should be in such

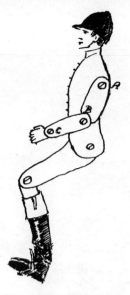

Fig. 13

a way that the two bones are parallel to each other and not twisted. Then the muscles and tendons are relaxed. If you imagine that your hands are made of three parts (like some mechanical doll), connected by some screws then undo the imaginary screws in A.B.C. and apply some oil so that those hands can move softly in a relaxed manner in those points. Make them loose.

This is the feeling that the rider must have when making contact with the horse's mouth.

Try to shut your fists and squeeze your fingers—you will notice that all the muscles of your arms are hard and stiff, and all those points, A, B, and C, are tightened. Open the fingers—you will feel the hands relaxed. Try to pull the reins by the hands bending in the wrists—you will notice that the muscles of your arms are stiff and the tendons in your wrist are tight. Passive hands do not pull; do not shut your fingers, or bend your wrist. They are just relaxed, attached to the mouth. They are so comfortable for

Captain O'Shea, member of the Irish Army Jumping Team in Rome, 1950. Note the remarkable sensitivity of the hands. The open fingers keep a light contact and do not interfere with the terrific effort made by the horse over a 6′ 4″ jump.

the horse that he does not mind the fact that they are attached to his mouth. When he moves his neck and head, for example, at the walk, he takes the rider's hands by this movement because the hands are so easy that they do not bother the horse. When the horse walks and moves his neck, the rider does not anticipate this movement, but his hands passively follow the horse's movement back and forward, *because the horse takes them.* The reins are at all times like a rubber string—tight but soft. This is the contact between the horse's mouth and the hands of the rider.

When the horse accepts the proper contact with the rider's hands, he adopts a certain position of the head and neck. He yields his jaw slightly and his head is inclined to approach the perpendicular line.

When the horse resists the contact, he stiffens his jaw and is inclined to approach the horizontal line. The snaffle slips into the corners of his mouth and does not act on his jaw. When the horse accepts the contact, he lowers his head slightly and stretches his neck. Then between the line of the reins and between the jaw and the neck, we can see a space, a sort of triangle. This is the position of the horse's head and neck which gives the rider the feeling that when he pulls his hands to stop the horse or to slow down the speed, the power which he produces goes through the horse's body in the direction to the horse's hips. And vice-versa: When the horse moves forward, the rider has a feeling that the pushing power of the horse runs parallel to the ground straight from the hops into the snaffle. The rider feels this power in his hands. In the case of resistance, when the horse raises his head and stiffens his jaw, the rider has the feeling that the power which he produces goes above the horse and the pushing power does not go parallel to the ground but somehow up.

If the horse resists the hands and overbends, the rider has

Fig. 14 Illustrating the two forces created by the horse and rider, meeting correctly.

the feeling that the pushing power goes somehow down, not forward. (The Dotted Line)

Action

To decrease the pace or to stop the horse, the rider acts with his hands. He pulls the reins in a straight line towards his *elbows as strongly as is necessary.* As soon as the horse obeys the order, the rider *stops pulling* and immediately returns to the previous passive contact. *Never start pulling with your fingers,* because you stiffen the tendons and

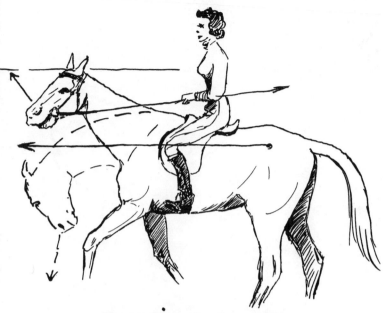

Fig. 15 Illustrating the opposite.

muscles, and the horse feels hard pressure in his mouth. Pull by your elbows, maintaining your fingers open, the wrist soft and straight.

Then the horse will feel soft pressure in his mouth and will not resist.

Resistance

There are, however, some moments when the rider has to make his hands hard and unpleasant for the horse. When we ride a horse which has been badly trained and does not want to accept contact with the rider's hands, instead of slightly yielding his jaw, he tries to push the hands away by jerking his head and neck forward and down or up. If we try to stop this, resisting with both hands, the horse might even pull us out of the saddle. To avoid this, we

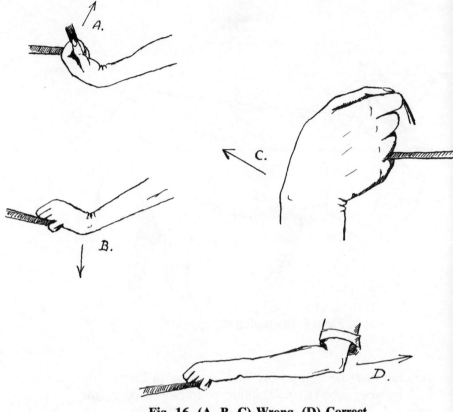

Fig. 16 (A, B, C) Wrong. (D) Correct.

shut the fingers and all those imaginary points A, B, and C, and make them hard and stiff, *but only of one hand.* The other stays soft and relaxed. Then the horse cannot pull our hands. He meets an unpleasant hard rein on one side of his mouth and punishes himself. In other words: *when the horse resists—we resist also, but only with one hand.* This is the only moment in riding when the rider makes his hand stiff. As soon as the horse's resistance vanishes, the hand *immediately* returns to its passive contact. The resis-

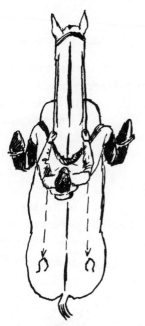

Fig. 17 Dotted lines illustrate the direction of the action of the rider's hands.

tance of the rider's hand should be only as strong as the resistance of the horse. Sometimes it is enough to tighten only A, without squeezing the fingers.

The power of the left hand acts on the left side of the horse's spine. The power of the right hand acts on the right. Those two powers act always in the direction of the horse's hind legs, never across his spine. Of course, when the horse is completely trained we can hold the reins in one hand and the horse should respond to the slightest movement of the hands.

The Legs

Analogically the rider uses his legs—before giving the order he gets in touch with the horse's body. He places his

legs so that they touch the horse's ribs just a little behind the
girth. The legs are relaxed. For all forward movements, the
rider presses the ribs of the horse with his calves in the
direction of his thighs by tightening the tendons under his
knees. The knees should never grip! (I will describe the
position of the legs when talking about the seat and position
of the rider.) The feet are placed well into the stirrups up
to the widest part of foot, heels down, and toes out so that
the feet and the upper part of the leg are in the same direction. The legs should always be in contact with the horse's
body. When the horse goes forward freely and willingly,
the legs do not act. They do not bother the horse.

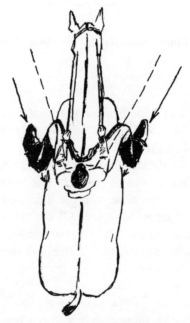

**Fig. 18 The arrows show the direction of the action of the
rider's legs.**

How the Legs Act

The legs act as strongly as necessary (as described above). As soon as the horse obeys, the legs stop acting and return to the previous passive contact with the horse's ribs. They act by pressing the horse's body, without changing their position.

To ask the horse simply to go forward, the pressure must be equal on both sides of the horse's body. If the horse does not obey the simple pressure of our legs, we give a kick with both legs at the same spot where we pressed. The kick is always much stronger than quiet pressure. This, one could compare with the hammer and nail. If we press a nail it does not move into wood, but knocking it with a hammer, we easily drive the nail into the timber with each stroke. When we press one leg behind the girth, the horse should yield his hindquarters in the opposite direction.

The horse on contact is not collected; he is framed between the calves of the legs and the hands of the rider.

Position of the Rider on the Horse's Back

To act freely with the hands and legs as is described above, the rider must be correctly placed on the horse's back so that he keeps his balance in all circumstances without depending upon the reins. All books describe the seat of the rider in detail, and they usually begin with, "The rider sits on the two bones of his seat, etc."

Here we differ entirely. We do not call it "seat"; we do not "sit" on horseback. We adopt a position which changes according to the horses' movements, which means that we must assure the horse's freedom in all his natural movements, while at the same time being able to control the horse under any circumstances. Where and how should the rider place himself on the horse's back so that the animal will hardly feel it?

If we compare the weight of our body with that of the horse, we can accept the fact that most riders are about six or up to eight times lighter than the horse. Some are even ten times lighter. If we know that the average horse weighs about 1000 pounds and the average rider weighs, including the saddle, about 150 pounds, the rider is about a seventh part of the weight of the horse. Now, let us take a seventh part of the rider's weight, or approximately 20 pounds, which would equal two or three bricks. Where should we place this weight on a man so that he will walk

Fig. 19 Illustrating the natural and artificial balance of a man carrying a weight.

freely without using his muscles?—*On his head!* Then the point of gravity of these bricks will fall on the same line as the point of gravity of the man. The man will not feel weight in his muscles. He will feel only pressure on his head. This is why people in Africa, Italy, or Jamaica, as well as the women in Albania, carry heavy loads on their heads. They move freely and with grace because the muscles of the body are not engaged in this work any more then is necessary. In Albania, we very often see a small lovely girl going gracefully uphill with a big basket on her head coming from the town to her home with her shopping. She is so free in her movements that on the way she is knitting a pullover for her husband in order not to waste time.

By the same token, the rider should place himself on the horse's back in such a way that his point of gravity will fall exactly in the line of gravity of the horse. Then, the horse does not feel the weight of the rider, and can move as he would without a rider on his back.

The old school, "classical dressage," changes the natural balance of the horse, moving it back nearer the hind legs, by bringing the horse's hind legs under his body and at the same time rising and shortening his neck. The horse is *collected*. This artificial silhouette of the horse needs a different position of the rider. The rider is always perpendicular and always sits in the same way; it does not matter whether the horse walks, trots or canters. The horse is not required to change his silhouette because he always works on flat ground without jumps or the other natural difficulties of cross country.

In "natural equitation" the horse is left in his natural balance and changes his silhouette according to necessity. *He is not collected.* The rider, adapting himself to the horse's efforts, *changes his position.* First of all he must take under consideration the effort of the horse's back. That

Fig. 20

Fig. 21

is why he does not sit on the bones of his seat; he just touches the saddle with his seat. He must sit this way so that most of his weight goes through his knees and stirrups. He must feel more pressure on his thighs than on the bones of his seat. The body is not perpendicular as in the dressage school. It is inclined forward, slightly in front of the perpendicular, ready to follow the forward movement.

From the horse's point of view this position is much more comfortable than the perpendicular seat of classical dressage because the rider does not change the natural balance of the horse. He adapts himself to the horse's movements, giving freedom to the action of the hindquarters as the pushing engine.

The horse in his natural balance could be compared with Figure 22. When the weight of the passenger goes through the axle, the boy who pulls the rickshaw does not feel any weight in his hands. Therefore he is able to use all his energy to run quickly. Similarly the horse left in his natural balance does not place any more weight on his hind legs than is necessary. He therefore uses them freely and pushes his body with the necessary strength without wasting energy.

Figure 23 could be compared with the artificial balance of the dressage horse, when his balance is moved nearer to the hind legs, and the hindquarters are overcharged; he loses the capacity to gallop fast or to use his hind legs freely. Similarly the rickshaw boy is overcharged by the weight of the passenger who is moved forward, towards his hands. He cannot run quickly because part of his energy is used for carrying the weight of the passenger, as though he was in a wheelbarrow.

The faster the horse goes, the more the body of the rider inclines forward, and the rider rises out of the saddle. This inclination comes from the hips. The back is straight; in

Fig. 22

Fig. 23

other words, naturally hollowed. The rider should have the feeling that he is approaching his navel to the horse's withers when inclining his body.

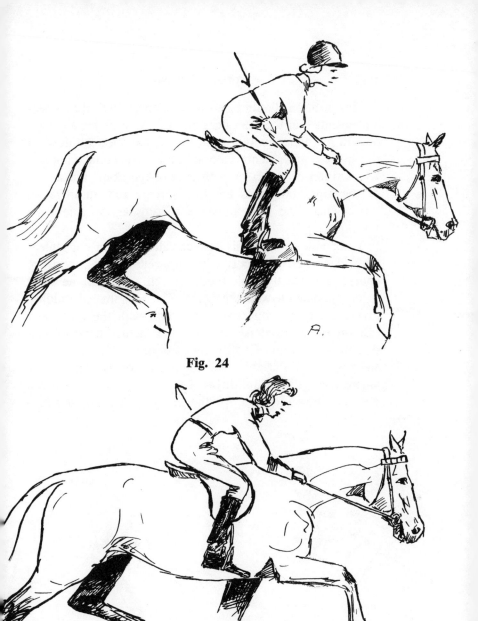

Fig. 24

This position should be so well balanced with the horse's movements that the rider does not need to look for any support in his hands or reins. He should be able to follow all the horse's movements without reins. We could compare the position of the rider with that of the skier, the angles of the hips and knees are like springs and amortize all movements. The rider uses the stirrups as the skier uses his skis.

To be able to have this perfect balance when not seated, the rider must use correctly adjusted stirrups, and, of course, a correctly built saddle which will help the rider in his connection with the horse. The best shaped saddles, giving the most wonderful connection with the horse and offering the best balance for the rider, is the "Pariani" saddle, made in Italy. English saddlers also make very good saddles of the Pariani type which are not as comfortable when new. (Like English britches, they are very good but are very uncomfortable for the first month.) Toptani sad-

Fig. 25 Points "A" and "B" act similarly in both cases.

dles are also very good, but some made in England have too much forward exaggeration. I mention the saddle before I describe the position of the rider in detail, because I consider it to be the most important part of the rider's equipment.

How the Saddle Should Be Built

The first principle is: the rider should be as close to the horse as possible. In other words, the padding should not be too thick. Just sufficient to give comfort to the horse's back.

Secondly, the knees of the rider should find natural support, and should be placed slightly above the points of the widest part of the horse's body, but the knees should always be close to the horse's body.

Thirdly, the correct position of the leg should be assured by the correct place of the stirrup leathers. They should hang along the balance line of the horse. Then the rider inclining the body forward and rising in his stirrups will be exactly in balance with the horse.

Fourthly, correctly adjusted stirrups should assure the immobile position of the rider's calves. It does not matter whether we jump, walk, or gallop fast, climb up or slide down hills, *the knees and the legs from the knees down should never move,* being always at the same place on the horse's ribs, *ready to act at any moment.* This is assured by a correctly made saddle and well adjusted stirrups.

After the last war, many riders started to jump big fences without having preliminary exercises in riding which would ensure proper balance. As a result, they had trouble keeping the knee and the leg in the proper position. The leg always escaped back at the jump and after the jump it was too late to resume the proper place to be ready to act if necessary. I have seen a top-class competitor in international jumping attach his stirrups to the girth to prevent his leg from escaping back.

People, particularly in France, started to build a special saddle, a real caricature of a saddle, with a terrific lump above the knee, and another big lump behind the leg to prevent the leg from escaping back. These are about the size of a loaf of army bread, and do not help the rider feel real balance.

In Germany, people began making similar saddles with smaller lumps. These still have too much padding under the knee. The French and German saddles push the knee too far down, thus making the rider sit like a fork. The saddle should not be flat. The lowest part should be in the middle.

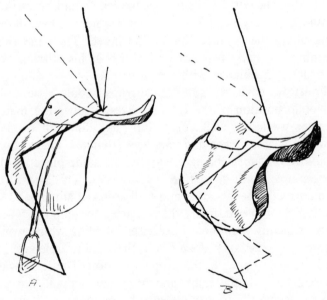

Fig. 26

Fig. 27

How to Adjust the Stirrups

The most important factor for the correct position is the length of the stirrups. When the stirrups are long, as in the "classical dressage" school, the rider must sit deeply in the saddle and cannot adapt himself to the movements of the horse. He can only amortize the shaking which he gets when sitting at the trot or the canter. The part of his leg from the hip to the knee is too straight down, and can not give the body support if the rider inclines forward. He must always sit straight.

When the stirrups are too short, the knee is too high and the calf cannot act freely and correctly, being too high and contracted.

Fig. 28

The stirrup is at its best length when the knee is placed slightly above the widest part of the horse's body, and the leg from the hip to the knee is directed more or less towards the horse's shoulder connection with the collar-bone.

When the rider places his knee and leg as above, and allows the lower part of his leg to hang freely, then the

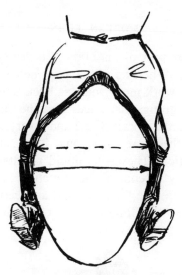

Fig. 29

stirrups should be one or two fingers below the ankle bone. The rider's feet should be placed with the widest part of the foot into the stirrups, in such a way as if he wanted to show the soles of his boots. The small toes should be a little higher than the big ones. Heels are down and toes out. This position of the foot assures the proper contact of the knee with the saddle and assists in giving the calves the required connection with the horse's ribs. We do not grip with our legs, except in an emergency moment. We touch the saddle with our legs, without effort. All muscles and tendons *should be relaxed,* then all movements are naturally graceful in full harmony with the horse.

The Position at the Walk

At the walk, the rider is sitting relaxed, easily touching the middle of the saddle with his seat. Every movement of the horse's back takes the hips of the rider in a forward motion. The upper part of his body is never behind the perpendicular line. When he passes over heavy ground where the horse must work more with his back muscles, the rider inclines more through the knees and the stirrups into the balance line of the horse. The hands, very relaxed, follow the stretch of the horse's neck and head, giving complete freedom of action. They still should maintain a light contact to be ready to control the direction. The legs at the walk are in touch with the horse and are ready to act. If the horse goes forward willingly, they are passive. If the horse

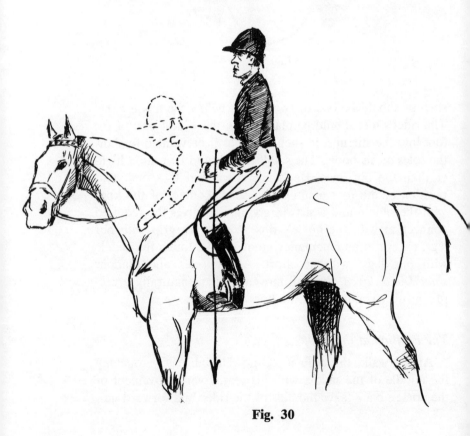

Fig. 30

becomes lazy, they act immediately pressing the horse forward.

To move on at the walk from a standstill, the rider presses both legs equally just behind the girth, and at the same time inclines the upper body forward. The hands are in passive contact, ready to follow the movement of the neck. The rider should never look down at the horse's mane. He should always look forward in order to direct his horse.

The Rider at the Trot

To facilitate the horse's efforts, we trot *always rising,* or as one calls it in America—"posting." Sometimes we use the sitting trot for a short moment when we have to act more strongly than usual with our legs. When sitting we are still inclined forward, in front of the perpendicular line so as not to put unnecessary weight on the loin muscles of the horse. As soon as we feel that the horse goes forward without hesitation we facilitate his work by rising every second step.

Here I would like to mention some historic facts about "posting." In Europe we call this way of trotting the "English trot" because it originated in England and came to the European continent during the time of the Franco-Prussian War in 1870. Until then, all cavalry used only the sitting trot with very long stirrups. The cavalry of West Europe marched only at the walk because the sitting trot for long distances was most uncomfortable for the rider as well as for the horse. The only cavalry in Europe which marched at the trot, even the fast trot was the Polish cavalry as far back as the 16th century, because the Poles rode with shorter stirrups and used a sort of half seat, balancing themselves above the saddle. (See "The Polish Rider at the Trot" by Rembrandt in the Frick Gallery, New York.) This sort of trotting we adopted from the Mongols whom we fought for two centuries. That is why the Polish cavalry was famous for being very fast.

I had in my library an article by Chief Instructor at the Vienna Riding Institute, written at the time when the new way of trotting arrived to the European continent. He wrote: "From England arrived a new idea of trotting on horseback. The rider is half the time above the horse and only half the time in the saddle. Apart from the fact that the rider is able to control the horse only half the time, this position is very dangerous because if the horse stumbles at the moment when the rider is above the saddle, the rider might fall off the horse and break his neck! Anyhow, I do not think there is a respectable horseman who would like to look like a monkey on horseback." However, some years later all the armies in their riding instruction adopted this English trot—"posting"—for marching long distances. This remark of a great horseman in that time seems silly to us today, but time brings changes and advances. And so time marches on! In 1926 our instruction for training the horse prescribed working young horses only at the rising trot, when trotting. I never used the sitting trot when retraining some very nervous or spoiled horses. Since 1926 I have never used the sitting trot and my horses are very relaxed and obedient, and they show an extremely attractive extended trot. The lighter the rider is on the horse's back, the more easily the horse goes forward. This old fashioned idea of always sitting at the trot and pushing the horse with the rider's seat and back is *nonsensical,* in my opinion. I was trained that way once upon a time, and my instructor, a pupil of the Vienna Institute, used to say that the rider should have such a push in his seat that he should be able to move a tram. This idea has been discarded. And so I have sold all my dressage saddles and bought two Pariani types made in Warsaw. I shortened my stirrups five holes and have trained hundreds of horses with better results. Now I train horses also for dressage up to Prix St. George standard, but I never change my saddle, my stirrups, or my position.

When we started to ride in our modern way, there were many voices of those conservative people exactly like the chief instructor in Vienna about "posting." They said we used a "monkey seat." This wonderful-for-horse-and-rider invention in riding was found out by chance. A postboy on an English carriage, who trotted miles and miles daily sitting and being shaken, perhaps one day after a good lunch and a couple of beers, proceeding on his journey, decided to rise every second step to avoid the shaking of his wonderful food and beer in his stomach. Others started to do the same. It did not shake the rider, and probably the horses went better too, and this spread throughout the world in spite of the disgust of many shortsighted authorities of equitation. *This happened a hundred years ago,* mind you! and today we still have authorities who write dressage programmes for three day events requiring the riders to do the sitting trot. Conservative judges ask the riders to carry out these programmes in long stirrups like in the time of Maria Theresa. The Polish three day event team never changed the length of the stirrups. We used the same position and the same stirrups throughout the whole three days—in dressage, in cross country, and in show jumping. Gustav Rau, the greatest German expert of riding, and judge in the Olympic Games in 1936 in Berlin, when writing about Polish riders in his book, says, "They know how to push the horse even when they do not sit in the lowest part of the saddle." We used the rising trot all the time and our horses showed terrific impulsion at the trot, especially the extended trot—*because we did not sit!* So we have still to win a battle with those authorities about the sitting trot, in the time of modern riding.

Let us return to the trot. I think that the first postman who started the rising trot did not think on which diagonal to rise and on which to sit in the saddle. The dressage authorities in the last years of the nineteenth century, having accepted the rising trot for riding instructions, had to approach this problem scientifically. The classical dressage school ruled at that time; horses had to be collected and under control. As we know, collection meant replacing the balance line (point of gravity) of the horse, back nearer to the hind legs. The hind legs were supposed to carry half or even more of the weight of the horse and the rider, as if the horse was a brother of the kangaroo. So one decided that in all turnings, let us say to the right, the rider should sit when the horse puts the right hind leg on the ground and rise when the horse puts the left hind leg on the ground. When the rider changes the direction, he should change the way of rising, so that when turning to the left, he will sit on the left hind leg. The changing was performed by bumping the poor back of the horse twice. In natural equitation, we do not collect the horse. The horse is left in his natural balance and his balance line is in its natural place nearer to the front legs, which nature created to support the greater part of the horse's body. That is why when we trot and we turn to the left, we sit when the horse puts his *left front leg* on the ground, and we rise when he puts his right front leg down. That way we are more in balance with the horse because the horse inclines his body into the turn, and we, adapting ourselves to his movement, incline with him. It helps the horse perform the circle and turn more easily. Inclining our body with the horse, we press the stirrup more on the side of inclination.

In the Berlin Olympic Games in 1936 in the dressage of the three day event, the judges honored our modern ideas and did not object to our posting on the inside front leg, provided that we changed when changing the direction. We change the leg (or rather diagonal) by rising two steps instead of bumping twice. This is easier for the horse, easier for the rider and more with the forward movement of the horse. It is so smooth that one hardly notices the change. And, in training the horse, one should not stick to one diagonal forever, because both diagonals should be equally developed.

Now, after the last war, in dressage competitions of the one or three day events, the judges simply insist that the rider should sit on the outside front leg, again as in the time of Franz Joseph.

To move the horse into the trot, the rider increases the pressure of his legs and inclines his body forward. The hands keep passive contact. The trained horse should start trotting in three steps from a standstill. To change from trot into the walk, we pull both hands equally until the horse changes into a walk, then the hands immediately return to passive contact. The legs do not act. They are passively in contact with the horse's body, ready to act. If the horse changes into the walk and starts to go too slowly or anticipates our order and wants to stop—the legs immediately press, asking the horse to go forward, and in that moment the hands are passive again on contact, ready to act.

The Rider at Canter and Gallop

As we mentioned when describing the horse, the back moves more at the canter and the gallop than at the trot or walk. Therefore, to facilitate the horse's effort the rider inclines forward and rises out of the saddle, and using the angles of his knees and his hips, he balances on the knees

Fig. 31 "Half seat" at fast gallop.

and stirrups above the back of the horse. The back of the rider must remain hollow with all muscles relaxed. The legs stay at the same place, heels down and toes out. This position I call the "half seat" (translating from our Polish description). The rider should always take the "half seat" when cantering a young horse in the beginning of his training, as well as while riding any horse in difficult country, on heavy ground, or at increased speed.

When cantering slowly while training the horse in the manege or in the paddock, the rider can take the full seat, especially when he needs to use his legs more strongly than usual. The full seat does not differ from the seat at the walk, except that at the canter when the horse starts his stride, the rider inclines his body more forward than at the walk, and when the horse finishes his stride the upper part of the rider's body returns to the perpendicular line. At this moment the body should never go behind the perpendicular, rather it should always be a little in front of it.

The legs are in the normal position in both the full seat and the half seat; the hands are in the same position as at the walk or the trot. When taking the half seat, the rider should shorten the reins slightly, because as the body is inclined forward, the hands move forward accordingly.

The half seat at the gallop was accepted officially by our army authorities only in 1928. I suggest using this name instead of the term the English use, namely, forward seat, because we have the forward seat all the time, even sitting at the walk, at the trot, posting, or sitting at the canter. The forward seat, I would say, is always when we use shorter stirrups and our body is in front of the perpendicular line.

Fig. 32 Full seat at canter (1) at beginning of the stride, and (2) at the end of the stride.

And in the old fashioned dressage, we use the *perpendicular seat,* which in some moments is even behind the perpendicular line. The stirrups are very long and the legs are stretched. The forward seat is the only position for the rider for modern sport and utility riding. The other might be good only for the circus.

Today, everybody accepts the forward seat in three day events, out hunting, and jumping. But still judges in dressage of three day events like to see the riders in the perpendicular seat with long stirrups, and so on. If the rider wants to have perfect style of natural equitation, he should *never change* his stirrups and his forward seat. The horse should be accustomed to the fact that the legs of the rider act always at the same spot, and that the balance of the rider's body should always be the same. We should stop forever this "dualism" in our riding. *No more riding in the archaic style of the 19th Century—dressage, and then jumping in the style of natural equitation, on the same horse.* However, I do think there is a place for dressage, and for the rider who enjoys riding dressage for its own sake.

How to Move the Horse into the Canter

The horse, as we know, canters or gallops leading with his right front or left front leg. When we canter or gallop cross country, out hunting, or during three day events, we do not bother about the leading leg. The only thing we are looking for is the direction and speed. How the horse puts his legs on the ground and which leg he uses to gallop is his business. But when we train the horse, we have to develop his muscles and their functions equally on both sides of the body. That is why we must teach the horse to respond equally to both leads according to our order. As we mentioned before, the horse has a very good memory. There-

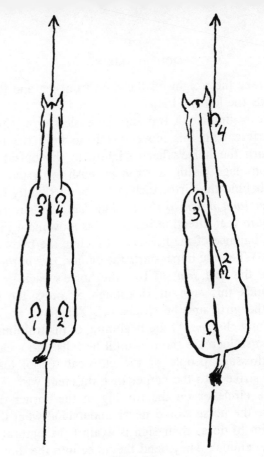

Fig. 33.

fore, when we train him to start cantering, let us say, from the trot leading with the right leg, we must use *exactly the same aids* every time we ask him to canter right. The sign should be easy for him to understand, and should not interfere with his natural position for starting the canter. As we know, the horse starts with the left hind leg, then puts down the left diagonal, then the right leading front leg, when cantering to the right. To facilitate this start, the horse uses his neck turning it a little to the outside (in this case, to the left) to take the weight off the right front leg and to direct it towards the left hind leg.

At the beginning of training the easiest sign which will not interfere with this movement is to hold the left rein (even turn the horse's head slightly to the outside), and press both legs giving a stronger push with the left leg slightly behind the girth. Incline the body slightly forward, *but never look down to the leading leg,* and never incline the body in that direction because this movement interferes with the balance of the horse. Just incline the body straight forward. When the horse starts the canter, *rise in the saddle* and take the *half seat,* to free the horse's back. When he understands this sign, it is enough to press the left leg behind the girth and he strikes off. The reins are passive without any change. At the beginning of his training let the young horse increase the trot until he falls into a canter.

The dressage people of the classical school teach the horse to strike into the canter in a different way. They do it on the circle or on the turning in the corner, because otherwise the horse would never understand what the rider wants him to do as their sign is against the natural behavior of the animal. They bend the horse into the direction of the leading leg, the head and neck turned slightly to the right (which naturally is opposite). Using the reins, they do not let the horse increase the speed of the trot. At the same time they push with the legs. Some schools give the impulse to start cantering using stronger pressures with the outside leg; some schools use for the same purpose the inside leg. As explanation, they say that the horse should always be straight at the moment of striking on into a canter, and when the outside leg presses stronger the horse might yield the hindquarters in the opposite direction. To prevent this they use the opposite rein, pulling slightly the head and neck into the same direction as the leading leg.

The other schools go even further and give the impulse by using the inside leg, which means in our case the right leg, to avoid the yielding of the hindquarters to the right. At the moment of starting the canter, they ease the right rein a little to give some, though very limited, freedom to the neck.

I think all this procedure is artificial for the horse and that he could never understand this indication on a straight line. Therefore, they ask it in the corner where the horse naturally inclines his whole body into the direction and must fall into the canter on the correct leg.

The aid which I recommend is natural for the horse and is understandable on the straight line without any difficulties. If you like, you can teach the horse to strike on into the canter to the right by knocking him on the right ear, for example, and to the left—on the left ear, and the horse after some time will do it. This is trick riding, and in natural equitation we try to give the horse signs which are logical following his natural movements.

In the Austrian cavalry before the First World War, the soldiers were in service four years. During the first period of training, the recruits had to ride with a stick two feet four inches long, held in the right hand together with the right rein. The point of the stick had to be level with the eyes of the rider and inclined a little forward.

After the first period of training there was usually inspection made by the general who was the commander of the division. It seemed that every superior officer in the army of Franz Josef II was always cross and domineering so that everyone around him was frightened to death. The slightest mistake noticed by the general was followed by an immediate "thunder storm." I have heard a fantastic story about such an inspection in one "K and K" (Koniglich und Keiserliche) dragoon regiment. Half a platoon, about 16 riders,

Fig. 34

entered the manege, riding in section one by one, with the distance of one length of the horse between the riders. All the recruits had the prescribed sticks. The general was in the middle of the manege, accompanied by the colonel, the adjutant, the squadron leader, and the platoon leader who reported his unit. The squadron leader is very self confident. He is the best rider and instructor in the regiment. He knows his recruits ride much better than the riders of the other squadrons. The inspection begins. "Walk." Everything goes well, the boots shining like a looking glass, bridles and saddles the same, horses groomed as though prepared for some wedding procession of a princess. The dragoons know their job. They look imperceptibly at their squadron leader, whose smile of approval encourages them. Some evolutions at the walk—perfect. Trot—the same. Everything is splendid. The general watches—no remarks, no shouting. "Canter to the right"—and suddenly something absolutely unexpected happens—one horse canters left! "Scandal," shouts the general. "Stop this schwienery, start again." "Canter, March." Everything starts smoothly, but the same horse canters left. "This is criminal," the general with a face red like a lobster with fury addresses the squadron leader. "The unit canters to the right and this blasted idiot canters to the left! Why?" No explanation. "Rauss!" shouts the general, and he does not even bother looking at the other platoons. The squadron for him is very bad. How could a war be won having one horse who does not gallop to the right! The squadron leader could not get over this. What a disgrace. And he had known this horse during several generations of recruits. He had always cantered correctly. What had happened?

"Sir," suddenly said the corporal-major, "it may be because I changed the rider. The recruit who usually has this horse is in the hospital and today another recruit rode this horse." "Give me the horse," ordered the squadron leader, angry like nothing on earth. He mounted the horse. He tried and tried to canter right and he could not do it. After about thirty minutes he finally got it. Still he could not understand what had happened to the horse who for several years always cantered correctly with the recruits.

A week later the "owner" of the horse returned from the hospital. The squadron leader watched the lesson. "Canter right," everybody canters correctly, no mistake. This horse without any trouble strikes on like a professor of dressage. "Halt!!! Come here, boy," orders the squadron leader. "Tell me what you do to start to canter to the right."

"Sir, if you promise not to cause me any trouble, I'll tell you the secret," answered the resolute dragoon.

"Come on, I promise. Tell me."

"You see, Sir, I paid ten cigarettes to the previous owner of this horse for the secret when I joined the squadron."

And he showed the stick to the captain; on the end which the rider holds in his right hand there was a nail.

"You see, Sir, when I want to canter right, I scratch the withers on the right side with this nail, and there is no mistake."

Several generations of recruits had ridden this old horse and probably for many years the riders used this trick sold for ten cigarettes from one recruit to another at the beginning of every year. The horse was trained in obedience "on the nail."

You can teach different tricks, as in a circus, but we try in natural equitation to use the signs which are as logical as possible. And there is only one logic: *Follow nature and adapt yourself to the natural movements of the horse.*

How to Change from Canter to Gallop

We use the same sign to increase the speed as is used at the trot. We act equally with both legs until the horse gains the speed we want. Then the legs stop acting and return to their stage of passive contact with the ribs of the horse. When we want to decrease the pace at the gallop, we just pull both reins until the horse attains the speed we need. Then again, the hands return to their passive contact with the mouth.

A well trained horse should keep the same pace even when the rider drops the reins. He should wait for the sign of our legs before increasing the pace. When the horse reaches this stage, riding begins to be a real pleasure.

How to Ask the Horse to Change from the Canter into the Trot or Walk

As we explained before, pulling both reins equally means decreasing the pace, but now we want to show the horse that he must trot. We are cantering at the speed of an ordinary trot. In other words, it will not be the case of decreasing the speed, rather it will be changing the way of putting the legs on the ground at the same speed. The sign given by our hands must differ from the sign for the decreasing of the pace. To change from the canter into the trot, we pull both reins but we start a split second earlier to pull the rein of the leading leg, which means when we canter right and want to trot, we pull both reins, but we start pulling the right rein a little sooner. We act with our hands as strongly as is necessary until the horse breaks into the trot. Then immediately the hands stop acting. The legs are passive but are ready to act if the horse should slow down and be about to break into a walk.

When we canter left, we start acting earlier with the left hand. This sign interferes with the action of the leading leg and shoulder, and the horse easily understands the rider's intention. A well trained horse in this way can easily change from a slow canter into an extended trot, which will be faster than the canter was at the moment of change. Of course, it is not of great importance whether the horse decreases his pace or not at the moment of change into the trot when we gallop cross country, out hunting, or on some other occasion, but it is teaching the horse to react precisely to the hands and legs of the rider. And, for the rider it is also training in precision.

To change the from the canter into the walk, we let the horse change into the trot using the above method, and then after two or three steps slow down into a walk. A well trained horse should be able to change straight into the walk. The action of the hands is the same as for the trot, except a little stronger. As soon as the horse changes into the walk, the hands stop acting, the legs are passive ready to act if the horse wants to stop.

When riding over rough country, we should facilitate our

horse's work by making ourselves as light as possible. The body is inclined forward and tries to be in balance with the horse, giving freedom to his back, his neck and head. Being above the saddle, the rider amortizes all movements, using the angles of his knees and hips. For his upper body those angles are like the "independent suspension" in a car. When sliding down, the rider should always be well forward and even rise slightly out of the saddle. The reins should be rather loose, the hands can take support on the neck; the heels should be kept well down, the position of the legs remains unchanged. Then the horse is not disturbed and slides down as though without a rider. If the rider sits back heavily in the saddle and holds the reins too tight, he presses the horse against the slope and scratches his hocks because he is unable to use them freely, being over-charged in his hindquarters by weight. When the rider behaves correctly on the slide, the horse has clean hocks behind. When the rider pulls the reins, the instructor immediately can tell which rider rode properly by looking at the horse's hocks. On very steep long slides, we walk or gallop. A well trained horse galloping down hill slows down, so that the rider having loose reins has to push the horse. It is at this moment that the rider gets this wonderful feeling of security. When we pull the reins too much going down at the gallop, the horse starts to pull against our hands and gradually goes faster and faster, like a barrel rolling down a hill, and at the bottom the horse might lose his balance and stumble, or even fall.

When walking on a very slippery and icy road, the rider should be careful to be easy on the horse's back. This is achieved by having loose reins giving complete freedom to the neck which the horse needs badly to balance himself. The body of the rider should be inclined well forward and his seat about an inch above the saddle. Then the horse is

as though without a rider and is able to use himself instinctively.

When we gallop in show jumping and the ground is very
slippery, we should be very careful not to use the inside

Mr. Ive Velge, one of the best Belgian riders, going over a 7'
spread, 5' 4" in height, at International show jumping in Brussels in 1961. The horse stood back, and in spite of being a little
late with his body, the rider gives complete freedom to the
horse's head and neck to save the dangerous situation. Notice
again the hands, with open fingers and the leg which has not
changed position.

(Photo—Y. Gollor, Brussels)

rein too strongly at the turning. We should rather let the horse bend his neck outside, which movement he makes naturally to keep his balance when turning. This means that we indicate the direction by discreet action of the inside rein and hold the outside rein quite firmly, then the horse does not slip. By pulling the inside rein too strongly we might turn the horse over. Before every sharp turning we should decrease the speed and then turn. *Never brake at the turn—always brake before turning.*

2.

The Rider's Moral Influence

We have talked about all the actions and reactions of the rider on horseback from the physical point of view, but as we stated before, modern riding is based on co-operation between the horse and rider. Full co-operation can be achieved only when those two bodies and nervous systems work together. The dispositions of all riders are not the same. One is the very excitable person, his actions and reactions are very quick, sometimes too abrupt. Being very impulsive, such a person very often acts too quickly and too strongly for a horse which is of the same nervous disposition. Another rider is slow in reaction, acts always a bit too late, does not concentrate sufficient energy in his actions. Some riders are very brave and determined, some not. By constant training, both types of riders can be improved. The quick nervous person can be trained to control his emotions and use only as much force and energy as is necessary. A good rider, in spite of his diabolic temperament, can be very calm, when his horse is getting nervous and excitable. The calmness of the rider influences the horse, who gains more confidence when he feels that there is nothing to fuss about, and starts to calm down. When the same rider gets on a lazy horse with very slow nervous reactions, he will awaken his horse by his temperament and will make him use his energy properly.

I am inclined to believe that between rider and horse there is some radar connection or some sort of radio communication between those two brains, because the horse reacts like a barometer to the disposition of the rider. One day a horse goes very well, is quiet, reacts well to all demands of his rider; another day the same horse shows excitement, his reactions are not as good, one can feel sort of suspicion in his whole behaviour. In most cases it is the rider's fault. The day when he is excited and somewhat nervous, he does not "feel" the horse well and all his actions and reactions lose their usual calmness and smoothness. When you train a young horse, or re-train an older one, and some trouble or some misunderstanding starts between you and the horse, your *first question* should be—Is it my fault? and if so—what am I doing wrong? Maybe I am too rough, maybe I asked too much, maybe the horse was too fresh and distracted so he did not pay enough attention to me and I did not have the patience to draw his attention to me. A good rider must be *patient* and *should never lose his temper*. He should always be able to *control his emotions*. I am talking about this from my own experience. I was a twenty-one year old lieutenant, keen in riding difficult horses. But I had very quick reactions and as well was very bad tempered. When I became cross, the blood somehow pumped into my head and I saw plenty of stars moving around and around. In such a moment I could not control my actions. Being an inexperienced rider, I never of course blamed myself. Once during a riding lesson, I rode a very difficult nervous spoiled horse, under the supervision of our colonel, a great rider and instructor. We worked about thirty minutes and the horse started to behave reasonably. Suddenly, I lost my patience and became cross. I jerked the horse and gave him a good kick with my spurs. Naturally, all the work of thirty minutes was gone. The colonel asked me to dismount and threw me out of the manege. After the lesson he called me to his office and had a long and very serious talk to me. He said, "If I see you losing your temper on horseback once more, I will transfer you to the infantry. You could be an excellent rider with your talent, but you spoil everything by your bad temper. *Be a gentleman on horseback* and not an uncivilized savage." I had to promise him that I would never lose my temper, and since then I have trained myself to control my nervous reactions. The colonel, to test me, gave me horses that were more and more difficult. Also, he gave me good advice, "If you feel that you are losing your temper, relax, give the horse loose reins, and just walk, or even stop. Do not work, just sit quietly and wait until your disposition becomes calm. Then take your reins and start to work again." This was an excellent education for me. After about nine years I was a different rider and a changed person. I learned how to control my temper. I was sent to our cavalry school of Equitation and it was at that time that my career as an international rider and instructor started. It is not enough to ride well-trained horses. To be a good rider, one must train young horses and re-train some badly spoiled ones. Then one gains a lot of experience and feeling for the horse, as well as the necessary knowledge.

3.

How to Train the Rider

We intend to produce in the shortest possible time a rider who will be able to ride a reasonably well-trained horse without any difficulty across any type of country and enjoy himself. He will be able to do so if;

(1) he keeps a correctly balanced position, and

(2) he knows how to use his legs, hands, and the weight of his body to control the horse.

During my long experience I have noticed that the temperament and the mental disposition of the rider are more important than his physical abilities. Of course, it is much easier to be trained in riding when one has legs proportionately long and the upper body slim, but I have known so many outstanding riders who have short thick legs and a comparatively heavy body. They had excellent mental dispositions such as courage, quick reflexes, feelings, patience, and consistency in their work. When the rider has a good mental disposition, he relaxes more easily, and this is a most important factor in all sport activities. Thus quicker and better results are achieved.

I have been asked frequently at what age is the best time to start riding. Naturally, youngsters are more easily trained than older people. However, I am against beginning too early, because it is difficult to find a suitable small mount. Small ponies, generally speaking, are not well-trained; some are very difficult. They pull and are disobedient. The small child has neither the knowledge nor the ability to control such a mount. As a result, the child gets wrong impressions and bad habits for which later one has to re-train. I am also against training children on big horses, even if they are well-trained. The child sits too high and his legs are too small and too short to be correctly placed on a horse which is too wide for them in the ribs. If the child falls off, he might be badly hurt because of the height. I think the best age to start riding is between 10 and 14. The child is big enough to ride a normal horse or to ride a pony of a larger size. I have known three men who started riding after 40 and became excellent riders. I know a lady in Brussels who started riding lessons after 60, and she rode every day in the Foret de Soigne, enjoying herself. The spirit and disposition of the rider, as I said, is the most important thing in riding. A great deal depends on the instructor too. A bad, inexperienced instructor can spoil the best disposition of the novice rider when he applies the lessons in the wrong way. He can discourage the rider, creating many difficulties. A good instructor encourages the rider, builds his confidence because he applies the exercises logically, and consequently avoids difficulties.

The first and the most important rule in training is— "avoid stiffening the rider and never ask the pupil to do something which is too difficult for him at the moment." Prepare him by giving some simple exercises which he can easily execute; when he has done them correctly and is relaxed, you can go farther. *Advance step by step.* To achieve quick results when teaching the beginner, you should have a well-trained and a very quiet horse. If you feel the horse is too fresh, lunge him before the lesson until he has lost his surplus energy.

The first lessons are very important. They must give the rider confidence and the feeling that riding is not a difficult or dangerous sport.

Never ride without stirrups, but very often without reins. Avoid fatiguing the rider. The pupil should finish his lesson relaxed but not tired. Therefore, the first lessons should not be longer than 30 or 40 minutes. Gradually they may be increased up to two hours.

SCHEDULE OF EXERCISES FOR THE RIDER

At a Standstill

(1) Put the pupil on horseback in the middle of the saddle. Be sure the muscles of the hips and legs are relaxed, the back straight and slightly hollowed.

(2) Place the leg in the correct position, the knee in the right spot of the saddle, the thigh directed towards the point of the shoulder.

(3) Adjust the stirrups. (This is covered in Part 2— The Rider).

(4) To avoid stiffness in the rider's body and to build his confidence, ask him to incline his body forward, at the same time petting the horse on the shoulder, on the neck, right up to the horse's ears.

(5) Then ask him to turn the trunk of his body to look backwards.

(6) Rotate the arms, together and one at a time.

(7) Ask the rider to change a glove or a cap from one

hand to the other behind his back, across his shoulders.

Apply these exercises at the beginning of every lesson for approximately ten minutes until the rider feels at home in the saddle.

(8) *Explain how to hold the reins:* Pick up the reins from the horse's neck and drop them, repeating this exercise until the movement is natural and relaxed.

(9) Explain how to shorten the reins and lengthen them: To shorten the left rein the rider takes the left rein behind the left hand, which holds the rein, using the thumb and finger of the right hand, which also holds the rein. Then the left hand slides forward as much as necessary; and vice versa. Repeat this movement until it is automatic.

(10) *Half seat and full seat:* Raise the body from the saddle, inclining it forward as if to post, balancing on the stirrups and the knee, above the saddle. Make sure the rider's heels are well pressed down, toes slightly out, and the outside of the foot in a higher position as if the rider wanted to show the sole of his boot, the spine slightly hollow. The rider should look in front of the horse, not at him.

(11) *Posting:* Practice the posting movement, which is rising and sitting with the body inclined forward. Do this with swinging arms, until a rhythm is established.

(12) *Show how to take contact with the horse's mouth:* The rider is sitting normally holding the reins in both hands. The instructor takes the reins about six inches from the horse's mouth and holds them pretending his hands are the mouth, thus feeling the tension of the rider's hands. He feels if the contact is stiff and hard, or too light, or if the hands are blocked by stiff shoulders, wrists or fingers, and accordingly he instructs the pupil. The correct contact should be maintained in spite of any movement of the horse's head or neck. He then moves his hands holding the reins so that the pupil may become accustomed to the vari-

ous movements of the horse's head and neck and can understand the idea of keeping the permanent contact.

(13) When you put the rider on horseback, first use a mounting block. Explain how to take the reins with the left hand, how to put the leg into the stirrup and how to place yourself into the saddle. Next show how to mount using the stirrup from the ground. If the horse is too high make the left stirrup five to six holes longer to be able correctly to mount the horse, then adjust the length of the stirrup.

At the Walk

(1) Explain to the rider how to move the horse from standstill to walk, and how to stop him from walk to a standstill; how to turn to the right, and how to turn to the left, as explained in the chapter on "The Rider."

Then you start the walk. If there is a group of novice riders in the lessons, there should be a trained rider on an experienced horse whom the beginners follow. If you have only one rider, then I suggest you put a lunge on the horse and walk with him. Ask the rider to ride wherever he wishes and follow him with the lunge. Watch how the rider behaves. If he is sure of himself, take the lunge off, but if he is not confident, keep working him using the lunge for as many lessons as necessary.

The beginner usually feels more confident if he has his first lessons in an enclosed paddock or manege. When he has gained confidence, permit him to ride in a larger field.

Be sure that the hands at the walk do not interfere with the movement of the horse's neck. From the first lesson, you teach the rider not to be stiff in the hands and wrists. The rider should maintain the same feeling he had with your hands when doing the above exercise at the stand still. The horse's head and neck should move freely up and down

My son, Anthony, at nine years of age, after six lessons, in Brussels, 1961. Notice how the boy follows the movement of the horse without depending too much on the reins.

(Photo—Dobrski)

and forward, taking the rider's hands, which are relaxed but maintain the same contact.

(2) Ask the rider to stop, and move on, stop and move on, right turn, left turn—repeating several times.

(3) Step over poles or cavaletti lying on the ground in different places. Draw the rider's attention to the natural movement of the horse's neck when he steps over the cavaletti. Explain how the rider should adapt himself to this natural movement of the horse. The horse, stepping over the cavaletti, stretches his neck down and uses his back muscles. The rider should incline his body forward, rising slightly out of the saddle, and his hands follow the stretch

of the neck. The legs remain in passive connection with the horse's body.

(4) While walking, drop the reins, pick them up, several times; also lengthen and shorten the reins, and repeat the same calisthenics which were done while at a standstill.

At the Trot

(1) First demonstrate to the pupil how to trot. Have the pupil observe you doing this. He is able to understand the movements more quickly. Demonstrate how to post at the trot. Permit the pupil to trot only short distances at a time, having him return to the walk at frequent intervals. I would suggest that another set of reins be attached to the noseband or the horse wear a neck strap for the beginner to use to help him get the rhythm of the trot and prevent any pulling on the horse's mouth.

(2) Trotting without reins: As soon as the rider gets the rhythm of the trot, have him repeat the same exercises as he did at the walk and the standstill.

(3) Trot over poles or cavaletti on the ground in different places. Then trot over cavaletti placed at five-foot intervals. Demonstrate to the pupil how he should behave while doing cavalletti work. The rider does not post—while trotting over the row of cavaletti five feet apart, he rises slightly and maintains a balanced position above the saddle.

(4) Change from walk to trot, change from trot to standstill, and from standstill to trot, etc.

(5) As soon as the rider trots reasonably well, posting, go out into a larger field. Riding in a big field or cross country gives the rider much more pleasure and much more confidence. Have the pupil walk to a designated point, then trot to another designated point, turn and walk, then stand still for, perhaps, the count of ten. This educates his activities on horseback. This exercise can be

varied to suit the terrain of the field. If there are no designated points in the field, use red and white flags (red for right turn, white for left turn.)

(6) *How to use one leg:* Demonstrate and ask pupil to do a *turn on the forehand*. Stop parallel to a wall or fence. Press the outside leg behind the girth, step by step turning the hind quarters around the front legs, which move but remain always in the same place, the inner foreleg acting as a pivot. The hands keep the horse from moving forward. The horse's head must remain in the correct position, the neck straight. If the horse does not respond to the pressure of the leg, the rider should assist by pulling slightly the outside rein. The leg presses with every step made by the horse.

(7) Next will be cavaletti at 21 foot intervals. This exercise consists of trotting serpentine between the cavaletti, making circles round them, making circles between them, and trotting over them while making circles.

(8) Next exercise will be double cavaletti at ten feet apart as "in and outs." Ask the rider to trot over them, and the horse naturally breaks into a canter after the first cavaletti.

After several exercises like this, explain to the pupil how to start his horse cantering and how he should behave at the canter.

Canter and Gallop

(1) After the row of "in and outs" of double cavaletti have the pupil maintain at the same speed. He assumes the half seat, or, in other words, maintains the same position as he used on the cavaletti. Again I suggest that the rider use another set of reins attached to the noseband, or catches the neck strap if he feels that he might lose balance. Canter no longer than 300 yards at a time.

(2) Explain and demonstrate to the pupil the transition from canter to trot, and from trot to canter. Then ask him to do it several times during the lesson.

(3) Explain how to increase and decrease the speed at the trot and canter; and ask the pupil to do it. This teaches the rider to use his hands and legs properly.

(4) Repeat the exercises described under the heading, *at the trot;* have the cavaletti two feet in height.

Riding in the Country

According to the progress of the rider, you should ride cross country, finding more and more difficult terrain in configuration, with banks, slides, hills, ploughed fields, boggy ground, crossing small streams, and so on. Ride in company with other horses, and ask the rider to leave the company and go alone at some distances from the others to assert his independence.

Gallop: Fast gallop, preferably in some big field or track where the gallop can be controlled by the instructor.

Jumping: Start to jump at the canter over small single fences of different shapes, up to three feet high. To further improve the activity of the rider, make the lessons on specially prepared courses. The course should include some fences at the gallop, some movement at the walk, including cavaletti at the walk, and jumping some fences out of the trot.

Canter without reins and do some exercises such as those done at the walk and trot. (See heading at *the walk.*)

Canter at full seat, changing from trot to canter, from walk to canter, and vice versa. Occasionally during the lessons have some gymkhana or games for variety and amusement.

PART III.
THE BASIC
COMBINED
TRAINING OF
THE HORSE

1.
General Remarks about Breaking In

Today most riders buy young horses already broken in. Very few break in horses by themselves.

The first period of training of a young horse is very important, because in this stage we should build the basis of confidence between the horse and rider and the principles of good manners. The better this is done, the further training goes without any trouble. But, by inexperienced handling and wrong treatment of the young horse, he can be spoiled so that more advanced training will cause a great deal of trouble even for a very good and a very experienced trainer who endeavours to re-train him.

Unfortunately, after the last world war, many young horses were broken in very badly. This is because there were very few people who knew how to break in a young horse without *breaking his spirit* or spoiling his confidence. Some people tried to go too quickly through this first and most important stage in the training of a young horse because they wanted to sell him as quickly as possible.

In our army instruction for the training of young horses, two months were allotted for the first stage. Of course, it is possible to train some horses more easily and the same results can be obtained in one month, especially when the trainer is very experienced. Some horses are more difficult, consequently one has to prolong this stage. We should, as a rule, *avoid a battle*. And we can avoid it by the progressive introduction of our demands to the horse only when he is prepared to understand, and by being very generous in rewarding every moment he did what we asked him to do correctly.

The horses of today are not born in wild primitive conditions like ages ago. Today, the horses from the time they first see the daylight are with human beings and therefore they are more or less tamed. They have much more confidence in man than in the time of being bred in natural conditions in a herd. One had to catch the youngster and separate him from his brothers. One had to put him into completely different surroundings—in a stable. It must have been a horrible experience for a free creature. This first experience did not help, of course, to build his confidence.

In most countries this first stage of training was based on using force to break the will of the horse. That is why, probably, in English we call this stage of training "breaking in." I would rather call it taming the horse. Towards the end of the sixteenth century the first riding academy was established in Naples. The first teacher was Griso, and his successor was his pupil Piguatelli. The training of the horse lasted five years. The horses were trained to be officers' chargers in the western cavalries. They had to have more or less the same movements as the Lippizaners in the Spanish High School in Vienna today. The method of training in

Naples was based on force. Therefore the horses had reputations of being bad tempered. No wonder. They had to defend themselves against the horrible experiences which they had to undergo during their period of training. The whole system was based on breaking the horse's will and spirit.

Before the last war, instructing in our cavalry school, I was ordered by our general to complete the library of the Equitation School. I tried to buy everything ever written about horses and their training in different languages. I collected many books written in French, German, Russian, English, Italian, and of course Polish. Amongst the very rare copies, I found in an antique shop a book written in old Polish and published in 1565!!! The book was written by some nobleman who did not give his name. He used "N.N." as a signature.

Mind you, it was published before the Academy in Naples was established.

This N.N. gentleman writes about how to train (he called it taming) a young horse for military purposes and for hunting. He also discussed how to train a dog and how to fish—three different chapters in the same book. Throughout the book, he shows tremendous experience, endless patience, and extraordinary logic about dealing with animals. His advice about handling the horse has not lost its value even today, after four centuries. He suggests to begin to train a young horse when he is three years old. At that time Polish horses were very well bred with a great deal of Arabian blood. I am inclined to advise waiting until the horse is four years old, except in the case of the thoroughbred, which can be taken into training earlier without doing him any harm. Remember that a half-bred gelding is fully grown when he is five or even six.

I will describe the advice of N.N. just for the sake of

interest. Perhaps it will give my readers some ideas and
opportunity to compare it with the methods of breaking in
young horses today as is done by some so-called horse
breakers.

When you catch a young horse, says Mr. N.N., you put
him into a box, close to an old trained horse. Try to think
how he feels. He was free, not bothered by anyone. He
could do as he pleased. Now he is closed in a small box
without his companions. Apart from the fright he had when
he was caught, he misses the company of his friends. He
knows that man did this to him. Do not expect this young
horse to have confidence in that man or in any man. So,
the best thing to do is to wait with great patience and tact,
and give him a chance to recover. Leave him alone, do
not bother him; give him hay and water and do not touch
him. But, do spend plenty of time with his neighbour,
groom him, caress him, give him carrots or something else
in such a way that can be observed by the youngster. This
will awaken his interest. He will see that you give the other
horse something to eat. He will see that the old horse does
not mind your company. He will start to pay more attention
to what is going on in the box beside him. After a time
he will decide to have a look. *When you tame a wild animal, do not approach him; wait until he approaches you.*
Of course, you must encourage it. In our case you encourage the young horse to come to you through your
friendship with the old horse. There will come a day when
this youngster will stretch his neck over the partition between the boxes and will try to approach you when you are
just giving a carrot to your old horse. Then is the time
when you gently, without looking at the young horse,
stretch out your hand toward him with a carrot. Some
youngsters will catch the carrot and escape. Some will take
it gently and stay at the same place. Confidence begins.

It might take several days. Do not lose your patience. *Wait*.

When the youngster behaves in a friendly way towards you, you can enter his box. It is then that friendship begins. Give him some carrots and gradually begin to touch him gently but firmly. When he seems to accept you, spend more and more time with him, playing with him, caressing him, and touching his body. If he does not object, you can groom him, first using just your hands, then straw, then a soft brush, and so on. At the same time you introduce the head collar. Many young horses are suspicious when you want to touch their ears. Do not worry. First put the collar onto the horse's neck, and while giving the food in the manger, try to attach a rope to the ring at the manger. If the horse shows suspicion, do not fix the rope to the ring. Just pull it through, so that the young horse can pull it when he is suspicious and starts to move back. *Always introduce new things before giving food*. For example put the collar on his neck, put food into the manger, and when he starts to eat, put the rope from the collar through the ring, and gradually try to fix it. Repeat this every time you give him food. The horse will understand that attaching him to the ring means food, and he will accept it without suspicion.

Mr. N.N. was against lunging the young horse. He thought the horse might struggle trying to free himself, and his young hocks might suffer. He prefers to mount an old horse and to lead the young one beside it. He starts this as soon as the youngster does not object to the bridle being on his head and the snaffle in his mouth. Before that he lets the young horse loose every day in a paddock close to the stable. He suggests to have such a paddock (corral) in front of the door of the stable, so that the youngster can be chased easily into the box after being exercised. When N.N. comes to the stage when he can put a bridle on his young horse, he takes him for a hack, riding a well trained older horse. He says that horses like to imitate or copy other horses. The good example of the older horse gives the youngster the idea about behaviour.

At the beginning he just walks quietly, leading the young horse. At first he goes on roads. Then he walks across country, across ploughed fields, up and down, and so on. According to the progress of a young horse, N.N. changes the country, creating conditions for the young horse so that he has to look where he is going and how to put his legs on the ground. Gradually he takes his pupil near places where there are different noises, to accustom him to different sounds and to traffic. Meanwhile, at the stable he introduces the surcingle to the young horse, putting it gently on his back, *always before giving him food*. He puts food in the manger and gently puts the girth on his back, leaving it until the horse eats. Next, he puts a blanket folded in four on the horse's back. If the horse does not object, he places the surcingle on top of it; the horse already knows the surcingle. Then the horse, dressed this way, gets his food. Next comes hacking with the blanket and the surcingle. The surcingle should never be tight. One should never provoke the objection which the young horse shows by blowing his stomach and stiffening himself.

Next is the introduction of the saddle. You show him the saddle, placing it in the box near the manger. The young horse looks at it, smells it, and then forgets about it. It is then you place it on his back on the blanket. With the saddle on his back, the horse eats his food. Then you take it off. The next step is to hack with the saddle on his back.

Meanwhile at the stable you introduce the mounting box into the horse's box. When he does not object to it, you place it close to him while he eats, and then stand on it petting him.

Fig. 35 Mounting box.

Horses do not like to have something or somebody higher than their back. They show suspicion. This must be introduced very slowly and carefully. When the horse does not mind you standing higher than he is, when he eats his food without noticing you, you put your arms across his back near the withers. Gradually you lie across the horse's back, always using the mounting box. When the young horse becomes accustomed to this, you get a young light rider to mount the horse. One must be very careful how the horse reacts to this. If he eats his oats quietly and does not resist, you permit the rider to mount. If the horse stops eating, stop any movement because this shows suspicion and he may do something unexpected. When he starts to eat again, proceed with the mounting. Usually the young horse prepared carefully does not object to the rider on his back. Now comes the most important moment of training the young horse under the rider. The horse must move with the weight of the rider on his back. He does not understand the action of the legs which later on give him the sign to move forward.

For a young horse, the first weight on his back is a very serious experience. That is why, before putting a rider on his back, we should use a saddle with a bag of sand, making it gradually heavier and heavier so that the horse will get used to some weight on his back. He will then be less sensitive when the *real* rider mounts him.

But the legs! The horse does not yet understand the touch of the rider's legs. So, when you mount the first time and you want to move, *do not use your legs.* Just sit and wait until the horse moves by himself with the first weight on his back. He may be coaxed with a bucket of oats. The rider sits passively without touching the ribs with his legs. He simply introduces weight on the horse's back. The horse should move by himself, following the oats. This is the moment when he begins to realize that the person on his back will not harm him or interfere with his movements.

Tell me, how may horsemen of today treat a young horse as Mr. N.N. did four hundred years ago, in a country where the horse was a part of the social life of the country, where the horse helped to make the history of a country which was at that time one of the greatest in Europe!

When the horse does not mind the weight of the rider on his back, Mr. N.N. takes him for an ordinary hack, but now with the rider mounted. The young horse is used to walking and trotting across country with the saddle and a bag with some sand. Now he has a real rider, who just stays on his back like the bag of sand, but he is easier because this rider tries to follow all the natural movements. When the horse walks and trots with the rider on his back, Mr. N.N. drops his lead rein, and permits the horse to go beside the older horse. Gradually, he asks the rider to ride the young horse farther and farther away from the old horse, up to about a hundred yards. And then begins the real training of a young horse under the rider, each with confidence in the other.

I think this first stage of training introduced by this N.N.

gentleman is excellent. We can follow his advice and I am sure we will never have any trouble with the young horse of today. I am inclined to suggest following the method of Mr. N.N. if you have an older well trained horse to help. I think his method is the most logical and most successful, if you follow the idea of his treatment of the young horse.

Lunging

In our army instruction, we spent a good deal of time in the first stage of training the young horse working him on the lunge, and I am very much in favor of this providing it is done correctly. Many trainers suggest a cavesson for use in lunging. It is sort of a head collar with a ring attached to a reinforced nosehead. The lunge is attached to the ring on the noseband. This is very good providing we use side reins.

Fig. 36

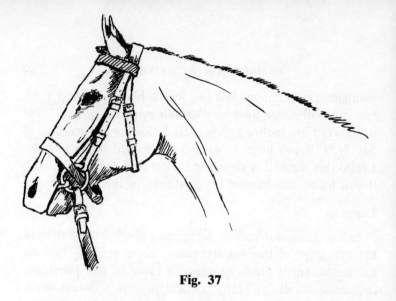

Fig. 37

If we lunge the young horse and intend to educate him in obedience, leaving him in his free and natural balance, we do not use side reins. The cavesson is very good providing we lunge the young horse in some enclosure where he is isolated from any provication or distractions. On the cavesson, if the horse wants to be disobedient and run away, he can do so easily, turning his head outside of the direction in which he is working and then by taking the lunge on his neck he can pull the trainer as much as he pleases. We are helpless because the horse pulls using his nose, and he can do it because there are no side reins to frame his neck in the straight position. Therefore, I prefer always to lunge horses in an ordinary snaffle, attaching the lunge to one ring of the snaffle. One can connect both rings of the snaffle by a strap under the horse's chin to prevent the snaffle from slipping on one side of the mouth, or put the noseband through the rings of the snaffle. This way I can control even the most disobedient horse and he cannot turn his head and neck because the lunge acts on his mouth, which is much more sensitive than his nose.

For lunging a young or spoiled older horse, I put an ordinary bridle with an ordinary snaffle on his head. I put the noseband, as mentioned above, through the rings but not too tightly. I take off the reins, and at the beginning I do not put a saddle on his back. I attach the lunge to the left ring of the snaffle, and hold the folded lunge in my right hand together with the whip. The left hand takes the lunge about one yard from the horse's mouth. I place myself beside the horse parallel to the front legs, facing the direction we intend to go. Using my voice, and whip (gently on the horse's shoulder), I invite him to walk. The left hand holds the lunge in contact with the snaffle. I walk with the horse leading him on a straight line. Then I turn gently to the left and so on. I walk about five minutes keeping the horse on a free walk forward on contact with my left hand. If the horse wants to run or play, I stop him using my left hand and my voice. I make the horse quiet and start to walk again. One must have a great deal of patience and lead the horse all over the place and in large circles until one feels that he understands that he is attached to the trainer and that it has to walk with him. When I feel that he marches easily, and is relaxed and obedient, I start to extend the lunge. That means I move from the horse leaving him on the previous track. Gradually, I lengthen the lunge to about three or four yards and guide him as before. The whip I hold is stretched towards the horse's hind quarters. In this way I come to the stage when the horse is framed in a sort of triangle. I am the top, the lunge is one side and the whip is the other side of the horse, which is the base of this triangle. When the horse travels all around the place and is obedient, I start to work him at the trot. He is obedient to my voice and to the gentle jerk of my left hand at the walk, so he is easier to control at the trot. When the horse keeps the pace at the trot and turns anywhere I like, I start to lead him over single cavaletti which are lying on the ground.

Of course, leading at the walk should be done on both sides. Remain on the left for about ten minutes, then change the lunge to the right ring of the snaffle and lead the horse to the right. Naturally, when I am on the right side of the horse, I hold the folded lunge with the whip in my left hand, and I lead the horse using my right hand.

I would like to emphasize one very important thing: The trainer, when lunging the horse, *must be very alert* in his movements and his reactions to the movements of the horse. He must always look at the eyes of the horse to be able to anticipate any unexpected movements. Very often, when starting to trot on the circle, the horse anticipates the turning, usually diminishing the circle in the direction of the stable or the gate. Diminishing the circle, he approaches the trainer. In this moment the trainer should very quickly shorten the lunge to maintain contact. The whip used in the area of the shoulder of the horse pushes him away. When the horse increases the arc of the circle forced by the whip, the trainer lets the lunge slip and keeping contact with the horse's mouth, guides him on the previous track. In other words, the trainer acts with the lunge like a fisherman, bringing in a big fish on a very thin line. If the fisherman loses contact and lets the line loose, the fish is able to give one jerk and is gone.

When the horse goes smoothly keeping the pace and does not anticipate the turnings, I ask him to increase and decrease the speed at the trot. I increase by using the whip behind the horse, and at the same time I move myself forward faster. I decrease by using my voice and slowing my pace. I always walk with the horse. When making a big circle or turning, I move in a small circle while the horse goes in a bigger one. I increase the speed at the trot always on a straight line. A well trained horse should stop when the trainer, using his voice at the same time, stops. The horse should stop and stand still without turning and coming to the trainer. If the horse turns, one should correct him, putting him quietly at the same place where he stopped. One should teach the horse from the beginning to wait for the order of the trainer.

When the horse keeps the speed at the trot on a big circle, I start him cantering, by using the whip behind him and at the same time clucking my tongue in the rhythm of the canter. At the canter I move in rhythm of the horse's stride in a small circle. To change into the trot, I use my voice and I slow down my walk until the horse understands. Gradually, the horse changes from trot to canter, and vice versa without hestitation. I do this in both directions.

Jumping on the lunge is very useful. The horse is undisturbed by the rider but he is still connected with the trainer and does everything listening to orders. For jumping on the lunge, I build the fences in a special way. The fence should be placed in such a way that the horse can be easily guided to it from a distance of at least 30 yards. I build the fence using cavaletti because they do not need standards. The fence for the first time should be small, two feet high and two feet wide, sort of double bar or double oxer. Of course, by now the horse knows the bars and cavaletti because he has trotted over them during every lesson. Now to invite the horse to make a jump, I build a small double oxer of the same cavaletti which are familiar to the horse. If I bring the horse to the jump being on his left side, I put a bar or pole on the left side of the fence to make a sort of wing which makes it easier to direct the horse to the fence.

Later on, when jumping bigger fences built of ordinary

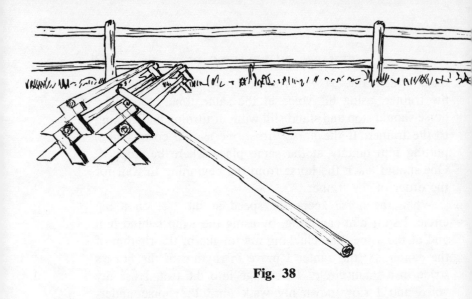

Fig. 38

standards and poles, I put a pole as a wing with one end on the standard so that the lunge can slip without being caught on it. The first jumps are from the trot. Gradually I ask the horse to gallop to the fence. The nearer he comes to the fence, the more careful I am not to disturb him. He must jump by himself. Of course, if he hesitates, I must use my whip to urge him forward.

I jump only young horses at the beginning of their training on the lunge, or very spoiled jumpers to build their confidence and to correct their approach and style. Otherwise, I always prefer training the jumper under the rider. After all, we must obtain total co-ordination of movement between the horse and the rider at the jump. So as soon as the young horse starts to execute the jumps over small fences, I suggest to carry on further training under the rider.

The Riding Ground

After one year of basic training the horse should be

obedient in speed and direction in all his natural gaits. This is possible only when the horse keeps his natural balance under the rider in all his movements. One can obtain this balance fully only by combining ordinary "dressage" (which I would rather call "ground work" so as not to confuse it with the classical dressage) with physical drill or gymnastics on fences.

The jump is a natural movement giving to the horse and rider a great deal of opportunity to exercise the natural balance. The horse changes his silhouette (see Chapter 2) and uses himself in a very drastic way and the rider has to adapt himself to be as easy as possible. Therefore, *we do not jump for the sake of jumping.* We introduce the whole method of jumping to the horse as a gymnastic which very systematically and gradually develops his suppleness and the co-ordination of movement between the rider and the horse. In the old classical dressage method we used a field or paddock about 200 feet by 100 feet, which was very flat. The going should be very comfortable for the horse, rather soft and springy. We do not need any fences. In modern equitation we use specially organized riding ground with necessary accessories such as cavaletti, fences, jumps, etc. The better we are equipped, the quicker and better results we will obtain. Our riding ground should have:

1. a flat comfortable place about 300 ft. x 100 ft.
2. an undulating place (up and down)
3. a place to put the jumps with the take-off higher or lower than the landing point (the best is the bank like picture)

and some fences which would be handy to put in any of those places mentioned above. It would be enough to have ten standards and thirty poles, and, above all cavaletti.

2.

Cavaletti

We started to apply this wonderful help in the training of our horses and riders in our cavalry school in Poland in 1931. It came to us from Pinerolo, the Italian Cavalry School. The idea was to construct a kind of fence, easy to move and to use in building different combinations of small fences, without using heavy standards and poles. Through years and years of experience, a certain system of using these little fences which everybody calls "cavaletti" has developed. By using cavaletti in certain ways, we train the horse to look where he should put his legs on the ground and to judge the effort he needs to negotiate them economically. At the same time he learns how to relax his mind and body and how to use only those muscles which are necessary for this movement and with the necessary strength. For the rider, the exercises on cavaletti give an opportunity to practise and obtain the correct balance and the correct position for the canter and jump, and for riding in rough country as well.

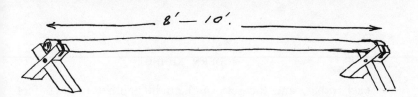

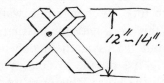

Fig. 39

The Shape of Cavaletti

Basically, it is a pole eight to ten feet long fixed at the ends to two crosses. When it stands on the ground it is one foot high. One cavaletti can be easily put on top of another. This way we can build fences of any height. Five cavaletti on top of each other form a fence of about five feet high.

Exercises on Cavaletti

1. We place the single cavaletti on the ground in different places in our field and we walk over them. When the horse is relaxed, he does not jump over them. He steps over quietly, stretching his neck and head to the ground as if he wanted to smell them. The rider inclines his body forward, rising a little out of the saddle. The hands, relaxed, let the reins be taken by the movements of the neck of the horse. When the horse walks quietly over the cavaletti, we do the same exercise at the trot. When the horse trots relaxed over them, we raise them to the normal height and we repeat the same exercise at the walk and at the trot.

2. We put five cavaletti in one row 21 feet apart from

each other, and the rest of them in another row 10 feet apart. We trot over them, straight and circulating between them, and we do our usual work at the trot, teaching the horse to turn, to change into walk, to stop, and so on, combining this work with the passing over the cavaletti.

3. We put the cavaletti in one row 5 feet apart from each other. First on the ground. We walk and trot over them. When the horse trots over them, taking each one in his stride, we can raise them to the normal height. Trotting over 10 to 12 cavaletti, each one foot high, five feet apart, up and down several times every day, makes the horse supple, relaxed, careful, and gives his muscles excellent exercise. The rider during this exercise keeps the half seat in full harmony with the horse's movements. The reins should be completely loose, to give complete freedom to the horse's neck in case he stumbles.

This exercise teaches the horse to be very careful and to pick up his legs. Many careless jumpers who had a habit of touching fences, after being exercised on cavaletti stop touching the fences and clear every jump very carefully. At the beginning they neglect the cavaletti and knock them with their hooves. The hooves, especially the front ones, are very sensitive. When the horse knocks the cavaletti it hurts him. So, after some time he comes to the conclusion that it is much better to pick up his legs a little higher to avoid touching. He remembers this when galloping over fences and is still more careful. Horses trained on cavaletti hardly ever touch fences.

4. We put every second cavaletti on top of each other. This forms a row of small fences two feet high and ten feet apart from each other. We trot and the horse starts to make the small jumps, in and out, taking the small fences at the stride as at the canter. The rider keeps the same position as before, the reins on light contact. If the

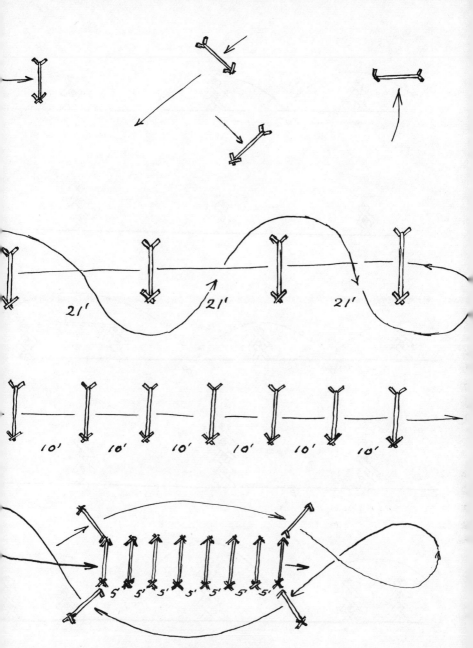

Fig. 40 Exercises 1, 2, and 3.

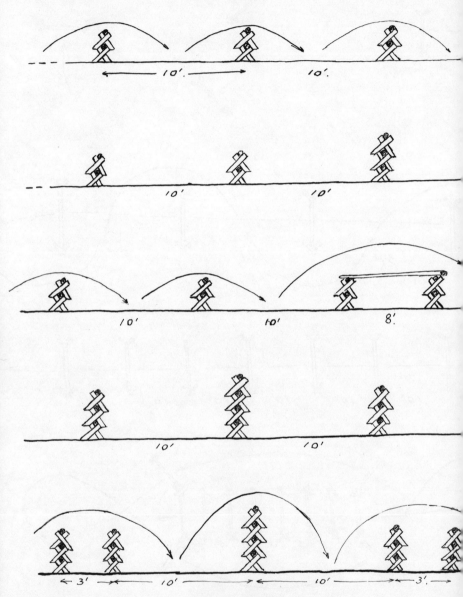

Fig. 41 Exercise 4, 5, 6.

horse hesitates the rider pushes him by his legs. If the horse goe freely and jumps willingly, the rider is passive.

Gradually we raise the last jump, putting three cavaletti on top of each other, and we jump it in both directions.

Without changing the distance between the cavaletti, we can raise the last fence up to four feet, or even four feet four inches, and repeat the same exercise. The horse learns to take off in the most economical way, folding his legs and using himself properly. To make still better use of his neck, we jump if from the opposite direction. This exercise teaches the horse to make a correct parabola over the jump and to use himself more economically.

To develop the attention of the horse, we make the height of the fences in the row irregular. For example, on every second one we put three cavaletti, and on the last four. The horse has to look carefully and to judge the height of the jumps and uses his effort accordingly.

5. To stretch the horse over a spread fence, we build a cube on the end and gradually we spread it up to 8 feet. However, the horse might jump into the cube. To avoid this, we put a pole across.

There can be many combinations built out of cavaletti. The trainer should use his imagination and apply them individually to the horses. I show here only the main ideas to make the horse careful and relaxed. For older horses who do not fold the hind legs enough I use the combination of three fences built of cavaletti: Exercise 6.

First fence—three cavaletti on top of each other
Second fence—four cavaletti on top of each other
Third fence—three cavaletti on top of each other
Distance—10 feet normally

This is a very difficult exercise which one can do with older horses just to correct the use of the hind legs over the jump. I use a still more difficult combination: Exercise 7.

First fence—a cube 3 feet wide, 3 feet high
Second fence—four cavaletti on top of each other
Third fence—a cube like the first
Distance—10 feet between the fences
We approach it at the trot. The horse has to make a good effort not to touch the middle one which is about four feet high.

3.
Jumping Exercises as Physical Drill and Obedience

When we come to the stage of training in which our horse trots obediently and correctly over a row of cavaletti five feet apart and jumps two placed on top of each other, we start at the same time to use a row of straight fences. We change the height according to the stage of the training and the age of the horse. We start from two feet and gradually with the older jumper we come up to four feet. Diagrams A, B, C, D, E, F, and G, are examples of how one should progress.

Exercise A.

We put four or five bars about 42 feet apart in one row. The bars are two feet high at the beginning. Gradually we raise them up to three feet. First we trot, circulating between them—see diagram A.1, 2. This exercise helps

163

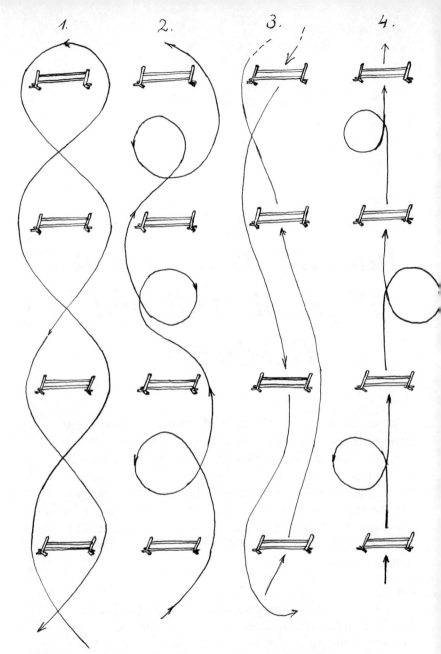

Fig. 42 Exercise A. Row of barres. Distance: 42'.

to turn the horse and teaches him obedience in directions. When the horse keeps the pace at the ordinary trot, we start to trot over single bars—see A.3 and A.4. After each jump we take him gently back to the trot. This exercise teaches the horse to obey the hands of the rider immediately after he has landed. Gradually he trots immediately after the rider gives him the sign. The rider should be able to act with his hands as soon as the horse touches the ground after the jump.

This work should be executed with great smoothness and without any rough jerks in the horse's mouth.

Exercise B.

When Exercise A is done smoothly and correctly, we start Exercise B.

Here we use the same fences but we place the first and second 42 feet apart and place the second, third, and forth 21 feet apart. That means there is one stride of canter between them when we approach at the speed of the trot. Then between the fourth and fifth, again 42 feet. We trot straight to the first fence. We jump it being in the direction of the other fences. After the jump we take the horse into the trot and we make a circle. Then we jump the next three fences. After the third we again return to the trot, we do a circle, and jump the fifth. Then we trot and stop.

We repeat this until the horse does it correctly. Then we do B.2, B.3, and B.4. This exercise gives the rider the feeling that he can stop or push his horse forward in any place or moment he wants.

Exercise C.

Next we put all five bars 21 feet apart and proceed following diagram C. 1, 2, 3, 4, 5, 6. One should apply exercises C.5 and C.6 only to older horses, especially to older

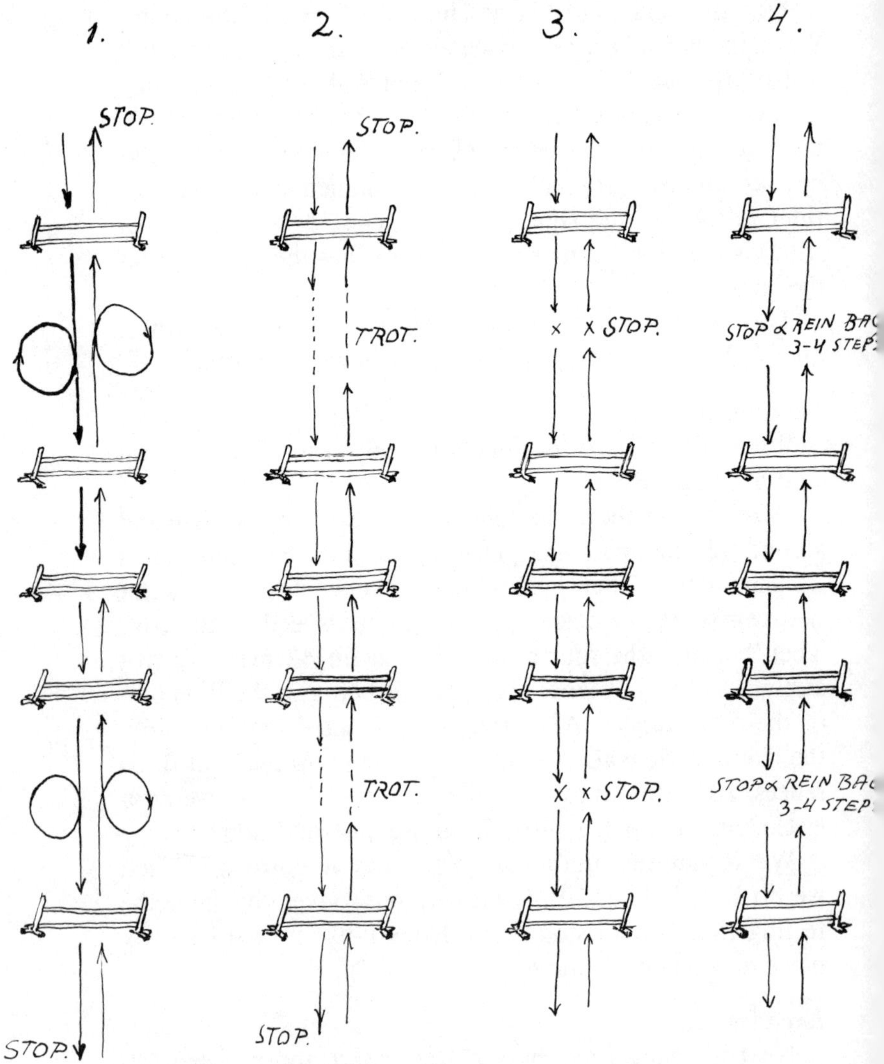

Fig. 43   Exercise B. Five barres in a row. Distance: 42′, 21′, 21′, 42′.

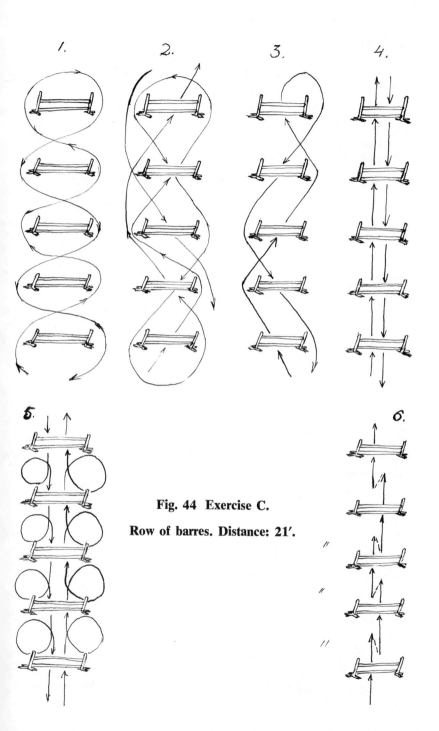

Fig. 44 Exercise C.

Row of barres. Distance: 21′.

jumpers when they rush to the fence and do not obey the control of the rider. We feel the extraordinary profit of this exercise when the fences are three and a half or four feet high. Of course, this must be done very gradually and not with a young horse. This exercise on fences four feet high is only for horses of international standard. Young horses should do it not higher than three feet.

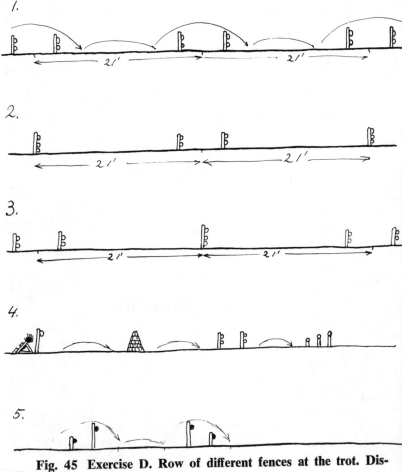

Fig. 45 Exercise D. Row of different fences at the trot. Distance:: 21'.

Exercise D. 1, 2, 3, 4, 5.

Introduce the horse to a variety of obstacles which he has to judge according to their shape and size. Again we approach at the trot and the distance between the obstacles is one stride of canter. We should measure the distance always from the highest point of the jump, to give the horse the chance to make an economic and correct arch over the jump.

Exercise E.

In our ground work when the horse canters correctly, i.e., keeps pace and balance and is obedient to our hands and legs, we can start jumping at the canter and then at the gallop. Every horse has his own pace at the canter in which he feels at his best when approaching a fence. Therefore, we should find this out and when galloping over fences we should let the horse approach at his own best pace. The length of stride at the free canter for the average horse is about 12 feet. So, for the canter, we place the fences 24 feet apart for one stride between them, 36 feet for two strides, and so on. For the first jump at the canter I suggest putting a small check fence at 24 feet distance before the fence to facilitate the horse's judgment of the distance (See Diagram E.1). For horses who rush to the fence, one can apply E.2, two check fences, as in and out, which will make him more careful. When the horse behaves normally, does not rush, and goes freely and calmly to the fence, we can exercise him on a row of fences as we did at the trot, except that the distance will be 24 feet instead of 21. Gradually, we introduce the row of different fences on different but regular distances, with perhaps one, two, or three strides between them. Jumping the row of fences on regular distances gives the horse confidence and the correct idea of the take-off. The approach could make a problem for him

1.

2.

3.

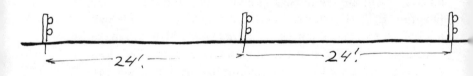

4.

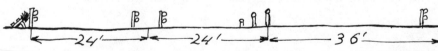

Fig. 46 Exercise E. At canter—row of fences. Distance: 24′ or 36′.

only at the first jump because the others are at a properly measured and prepared distance.

Exercise F.

Now comes the moment when the horse should learn the approach to the fence for himself. He should judge the size of the fence and the distance to the point of take-off. To draw his attention to the fence and to make him careful, we build the fences in such a way so that they can be changed every time the horse approaches. For the first exercise of this kind, we build two cubes and place hooks on the standards according to the height we intend to jump as the exercise progresses. For this we need four standards and four poles for each fence. Eight standards and eight poles altogether. We prepare these standards in such a way that the poles can be easily placed at the desired height. The rider gallops at the pace which the horse likes best, usually a moderate gallop, and keeps the same pace at all times. His business is to keep the pace and to direct the horse straight to the jump, without any interference. He gives the order to jump by directing the horse into the middle of the fence, and when the horse approaches leaves him alone. Allow him to make the mistakes. The more mistakes the horse makes, the better he learns to approach properly. He must do it by himself without being dictated to by the rider.

We put two poles on the first standards about two feet high. As soon as the horse has jumped this, we put a third pole on the second pair of standards, making a small cube. The horse approaching the same jump a second time suddenly notices that there is some change. He pricks his ears and watches carefully. After he jumps this, we place a third bar from the second pair of standards on the first pair, making a straight bar, but one foot higher. Of course, the horse notices this and jumps carefully. After he jumps this,

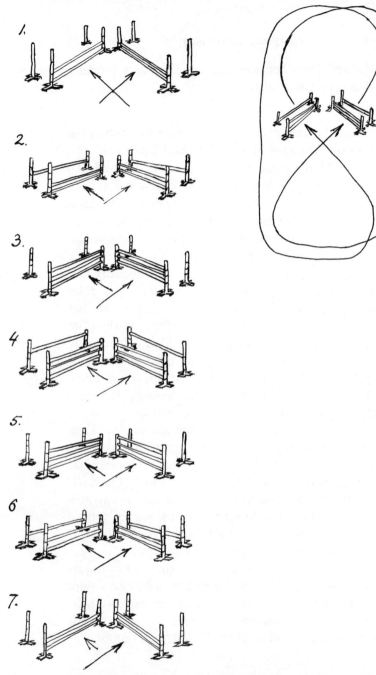

Fig. 47 Exercise F. Approach. Diagram 8 shows the way of approaching the fences, which are changed as in diagrams 1-7.

we make a double bar or cube still higher, putting another pole on the second pair of standards.

Next, we make the fences lower, gradually coming to the same height which we started with. In other words, we gradually make the jumps higher and larger and then gradually diminish them to the size we used at the beginning of our lesson. The size depends on the age of our horse and the stage of his training.

In the further stages of training our jumper, we put these fences in such a way that the first is a straight fence of three bars, and the next is a triple bar of the same height but, let us say, with a six foot spread. From afar, the three bars put up as a straight fence and the three bars as a triple bar look the same. Only when approaching closer does the horse realize that there is a difference. Of course, when giving the order to jump the big triple bar, the rider gradually increases the pace, which indicates to the horse that it must be a big spread and not a perpendicular fence.

Even the best trainers with the best horses sometimes make mistakes, because each horse reacts individually to all these exercises.

I remember, I applied almost the same training to my best horses which were the last I had before the war, Ben Hur and Abdel Krim. Ben Hur followed all the instructions without any trouble. Finally he won the championship of Poland for the three day event for two years in succession. (He gave his life defending his country.) Abdel Krim was one of our best show jumpers, but there was a time when suddenly he became so careful in approaching that he started to check himself in front of the fence so much that in spite of my push he lost his impulse. This was very troublesome especially when approaching big spreads. I decided to put him into the biggest army point-to-point races, to encourage him behind other horses in speed races. He won

Myself—demonstrating during a lesson. The legs do not change their position, and the hands are relaxed and light, with open fingers.

(Photo—A. Dobrski, Brussels)

This is how NOT to do it.

both the races he ran and this experience helped him very much. After that he went to the fence without any hesitation, judging the distance perfectly. I took him to our international jumping contest in Warsaw and he won the first competition. He beat the best French, German, and other European horses. He was also the most beautiful and powerful jumper I ever had.

Applying all these exercises on cavaletti and other fences, we should be able to train the average horse correctly. Next comes experience, which gives the horse the ability to jump big fences at the fast gallop. In other words: First we must obtain the technique of the jump, and then comes speed and "puissance."

Before we start to jump at the center, we could apply

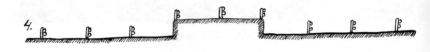

Exercise 6, at the trot, which gives the horse great suppleness and balance. Of course, this is possible if we have a bank about three feet high and 21 feet wide. Then, using our ordinary cavaletti we apply extraordinary gymnastics for the horse and rider. Using another type of bank, we can apply exercises G.5, 6, and 7.

When the horse knows how to jump fences on the level ground at the canter, we should apply Exercise G at the canter.

The horse should be balanced not only when jumping on flat ground, but also jumping fences when the take-off point and landing are not on the same level. Of course, one should combine jumps over bars with jumps over ditches with or without water in them .

How Much Should We Jump?

To learn how to jump and to obtain a proper style, we must jump a good deal. We must jump every day, but small jumps two feet or maximum three feet high. These small jumps do not harm the horse. Imagine that the legs of every horse are more than three feet high. If the horse bends his legs properly, his body is not lifted more than a couple of inches when jumping over small fences of two to three feet high. At such jumps, the horse does not make more effort than at the ordinary stride of the canter. So we can jump many small jumps every lesson, up to perhaps 60, but the higher and bigger the fences are, the less we should jump. When we come to a stage when the fences are three and a half feet high, then we jump every second day and not more than 20 or 30 jumps during the lesson.

Fig. 48 Exercise G. Cavaletti or bars combined with bank, landing higher or lower than the take off. Diagrams 1-4 at the trot, 5-7 at the canter.

PROGRAM FOR TWELVE MONTHS
COMBINED TRAINING OF A YOUNG HORSE

At the end of a year of training, the horse should be easy to control on a plain snaffle at all natural gaits, alone or in the company of other horses, on flat or over rough country, being, under all conditions, quiet and relaxed. Stages: To be able to progress, controlling the horse's progress, we divide the whole training into three stages.

FIRST STAGE: About two months (this is the "breaking in" or taming period).

During this stage the horse has to become accustomed to the new conditions of his life in the stable, such as feeding, grooming, confidence in people, the bridle and the saddle. He has to learn to stand still when mounted and dismounted, and to carry the weight of the rider at the walk and at

M. Richard Aden (16 year old rider) at a trial jump in front of the General Secretary of the F. E. I.

the trot, going willingly forward on the straight lines. Some horses who are making good progress can also do the same at a free canter, but not farther than 200-300 yards at a time.

SECOND STAGE: about four months.

At this stage the horse should accept proper contact with the rider's hands and legs at the walk and at the trot. He should know (a) how to keep the tempo at the trot; (b) he should be able to turn easily and to make circles of about ten yards diameter at the walk and at the trot; (c) he should easily move from a standstill into a walk, from a walk into a trot, and change from trot into walk and halt; (d) he should stand still, immobile, and be able to turn on the forehand; (e) he should canter on the correct lead from the trot and should be able to increase and decrease his pace at the trot.

THIRD STAGE: about six months.

At this stage we should obtain the total control of the horse at all natural gaits. He should be handy, should change easily from one gait to another, and should rein back. He should change the pace at the trot and at canter or gallop. He should know the extended trot.

I STAGE: First Month.
A. *The Ground Work.*
1. Accustom the horse to the bridle.
2. Lunge him.
3. Accustom the horse to the saddle.
4. Lunge him with the saddle on his back at the walk, trot, and canter.
5. Mount and dismount.
6. Lead him under a rider.
7. Walk free on straight line under a rider.

Remarks: Pay attention to the correct adjustment of the snaffle. Make the bridle slightly bigger than is necessary, to avoid any trouble when putting it on the horse's head for the first time. Then adjust it correctly. Do not pull the girth too tight, leave it rather loose when saddling the horse for the first time. The first mounting outdoors should be done at the end of the lunging lesson. Have some oats in a basket and give them to the horse as the rider mounts. The rider should not move. Let the horse stand still and eat the oats. Then invite the horse to follow you, moving and coaxing him with the oats. Then lead the horse at the walk, watching how he behaves. When the horse does not mind, or pay any attention to the presence of the rider on his back, take the lunge off and walk beside him, gradually leaving him alone. The rider should sit very lightly, using his hands and voice very gently. The rider should avoid using his legs until he is sure that the horse does not mind their touch.

B. *Jumping Exercises.*

1. Step over single cavaletti on the ground at the walk and trot on the lunge.
2. Do the same over cavaletti one foot high.
3. Do the same over little cubes one foot high and two feet wide.

Remarks: Do these exercises at the end of the lunging lesson. Put the cavaletti against a wall or a fence of the paddock and use another cavaletti a foot high as a wing, to avoid any attempts of disobedience. The first time, lead the horse over the cavaletti, stepping over it at the same time as he does. Gradually lunge the horse over the cavaletti.

I STAGE: Second Month.

A. *The Ground Work.*

1. Free walk on straight lines.
2. Trot on straight lines.

3. Changes of direction.
4. Ride in open country in the company of other older, well-trained horses.
5. Free movement forward at the trot and walk.
6. Free canter on a straight line, not farther than 200-300 yards.

Remarks: From the beginning, make the horse go forward willingly. Use your voice and stick more than the legs. The trot at the beginning should also be faster than ordinary. The contact with the horse's mouth should be very light, very gentle. At the beginning, the reins should be rather loose. When the horse goes forward willingly and freely, then try to take only light contact. The neck should be stretched and lower than is normal. When the horse's back becomes accustomed to the weight of the rider, the horse will raise his neck to its normal position and will use it normally without the contraction of the muscles. Avoid making sharp turns when changing the direction. Do not forget to change the diagonal at posting. When changing from the trot to the walk, use your voice more than your hands. Use your hands gently so as not to provoke the contraction of the neck, or any opposition in the mouth.

The first ride in open country should be easy for the horse. The ground should not be heavy and should be flat. Gradually ride across undulating ground at the walk. Trot only on flat ground. Take the half seat when cantering. Do not mind on which leg the horse canters. Just let him become accustomed to the rider's weight at this natural movement. Ride in the open country as often as possible, two or three times in a week.

B. *The Jumping Exercises.*
1. Walk over cavaletti on the ground. (See exercise on cavaletti N.1, 2.)
2. Trot doing the same exercises.

Remarks: Approaching the cavaletti, give the horse the direction from at least ten yards in a straight line. Maintain the straight line after the cavaletti for at least ten to twenty yards.

II STAGE: First Month.

A. *The Ground Work.*
1. Put the horse on steady pace (rhythm) at the walk.
2. Put the horse on steady pace at the trot (tempo).
3. Begin the handiness at the walk and at the trot; turnings, changes of direction, and circles.
4. Transition from walk to trot, and vice versa.
5. Halt from walk, and standstill.
6. Cantering—as was done at the first stage.

Remarks: Still begin the lessons by lunging the horse, especially if he is excitable. At the begnning of this stage you should very gently and gradually introduce the contact to the horse. First of all, be sure that the horse moves forward with natural impulsion.

B. *The Jumping Exercises.*
1. Repeat the exercises on cavaletti N.1, 2 at the walk and at the trot.
2. When the horse does this correctly, proceed to exercise N.3 on the ground.
3. Trot over different small (1 foot 6 inches = 2 feet) fences, such as colored poles, stone wall, small cubes built of colored poles.

Remarks: Apply the jumping exercises every lesson on the riding ground. At least once a week ride in the country. Walk over undulating ground. Trot and canter on the flat. Every lesson should finish by walking at least ten minutes to bring the horse to the stable calm and cool. The horse should finish his daily work relaxed, but not tired.

II STAGE: Second Month.

**Miss Joan Sellers (16 years old) on The Huguenot, during a
lesson in Winnipeg, Canada.**

(Photo—Miss E. Geiger)

A. *The Ground Work.*

1. Further improvement of the handiness at the walk and at the trot. Improvement of the contact and the reaction to the rider's hands and legs. Increasing and decreasing the pace at the trot, transistion from trot to walk and stop, and vice versa.
2. Cantering, as was done before.
3. If the horse stands still and quiet, do turning on the forehand. (See page 97 point 6.)

Remarks: Lunge at the walk, trot, and canter. When doing the increasing and decreasing of pace at the trot, take care to execute it smoothly and do not ask too much at the beginning. When decreasing the pace, do not make abrupt actions with the hands which might provoke the horse's resistance. Riding cross country, walk and trot over undulating ground.

B. *The Jumping Exercises.*

1. Repeat the work of the previous month.
2. Cavaletti, exercise N.3, raise up to one foot.
3. The single fences at the trot, up to two feet.
4. Exercises on cavaletti, N.4.

Remarks: Apply the exercise N.4 only when the horse trots correctly over the row of cavaletti at five feet apart, and jumps at the trot over the single fences two feet high. Then apply ins and outs, starting with two, then three.

II STAGE: Third Month.

A. *The Ground Work.*

1. Work at the walk and trot as before. Make the turning of circles, half circles and serpentine more precisely, diminishing the diameter up to 30 feet.
2. Halt from walk and from trot.
3. Stand still for at least 20 seconds.
4. Turn on the forehand.

5. Canter on the correct lead out of the trot on large circles and on the straight line.

Remarks: When the horse canters correctly, start to accustom him to the full seat.

B. *The Jumping Exercises.*
1. Cavaletti as before.
2. Use the row of fences exercises A.1, 2, and 3, not higher than two feet.
3. Single fences at the trot up to two feet four inches.

Remarks: When trotting over single fences, be careful that the horse does not lose his forward impulse. Let him break into the canter if he is so inclined. The horse should go willingly to the fence without rushing. Hack in the country over various types of ground, with other horses if possible. Pass small ditches and other small fences, if possible following an experienced older horse.

II STAGE: Fourth Month.

A. *The Ground Work.*
1. Further perfecting of the exercises of the previous month.
2. Transition from trot to canter, and vice versa.

Remarks: If you have the opportunity to train your horse in the company of other horses, train him to stand still as the other horses pass by.

B. *The Jumping Exercises.*
1. Cavaletti as was done before, exercises N. 3 and 4.
2. Row of fences at the trot, exercise A.1, 2, 3 and exercise C.1, 2 and 4.
3. Canter over single fences.

Remarks: The row of three fences at the beginning, when the horse goes willingly and jumps three fences keeping the direction without trouble, may be adjusted by raising the last fence up to three feet. At the end of this month, if the horse keeps the pace at the canter, you may start cantering over small single fences two feet high. If the horse does not yet keep the pace at the canter, continue to jump at the trot only.

The example of the lesson at the end of this stage:

10 - 15 minutes walk:

Free walk on loose rein, walk on contact, take contact, and give loose rein several times. Several times stop and stand still, on contact and on loose rein. Changing the directions, circles, half circles, serpentine between the fences, walk over cavaletti (single and row).

15 - 20 minutes trot:

Free trot on light contact. After 5 minutes put the horse on steady pace at the slow trot. Take him on proper contact and do circles, half circles, serpentines between the fences. Trot over the row of cavaletti. Make the transition from trot into walk, and vice versa. Halt from trot and move into trot out of halt. When the horse does this well, give him a rest on loose rein at the walk. Then start trotting again on contact and increase and decrease the speed at the trot.

2 - 5 minutes rest (loose reins at the walk).

5 minutes walk on contact, halt and turn on the forehand several times in both directions.

5 minutes start cantering at half seat, put the horse on steady free pace and do big turnings and big circles, keeping the same pace all the time.

Change the direction at the trot and start the same on the other leading leg.

1 - 2 minutes rest.

10 minutes striking on at the canter from the trot. Do not canter more than 15 - 20 strides. After changing into the trot, put the horse in a steady even slow trot and do not canter until he is well balanced at the trot.

Repeat this several times once to the left, once to the right.
1 minute rest.
10 minutes trotting over the fences single and in a row.
10 minutes free walk on loose rein.

III STAGE: First Month.
A. The Ground Work.

1. Train the horse at the walk and at the trot as was done in the end of the previous stage, perfecting the handiness and the transitions from one gait to another; perfect the standstill and the turning on the forehand.
2. Start the handiness at the canter; using the full seat do circles gradually smaller and smaller up to 30 foot diameter.
3. Reining back.

Remarks: When making the circles, pay attention to keeping the neck of the horse straight, so that the hind legs follow the front legs. Ride in open country over rough ground. Walk in and out of dry ditches. Ride in staggered formation in company and alone. Open gates, etc., mount and dismount.

B. The Jumping Exercises.

To improve the style and obedience of the horse, exercises B.1, 2, 3, 4; C.3, 4; D.1.

Cavaletti exercise 3. exercise 4. raising last up to three cavaletti. At the canter jump single varied fences with check fence 24 feet or 36 feet in front to give the horse the correct idea of approach.

Remarks: Cavaletti — every day.
Jumping every second day.

III STAGE: Second Month.
A. The Ground Work.

1. Work as was done in the previous month.
2. Gradually diminish the size of the turnings and the circles at the center.
3. Transitions from walk into canter, and from canter into trot and walk and halt.
4. Reining back.

Remarks: Remember to keep the horse's neck straight when doing small circles so that he uses his hocks. The small circles at the canter prepare the horse to turn at the canter on the hocks (pirouette). This is an excellent exercise for the hindquarters, and makes the horse very agile.

B. *The Jumping Exercises.*

1: Cavaletti as usual.
2. Row of fences at the trot as before.
3. At canter, exercise F up to three feet.

Remarks: Raise the row of fences at the trot up to three feet always keeping in mind the importance of obedience to the hands and legs, and at the same time the development of the correct style over the jump.

III STAGE: Third Month.

A. *The Ground Work.*

Further improvement of the work of the previous month. Gradually diminish the turnings and circles. Changing of the leading leg at the center, with transistion to the trot, then to the walk, then to halt. Extended trot.

Remarks: When teaching the horse the changing of the lead at the canter with the transition to the trot, pay attention that the transition is smooth and that the trot is steady and rhythmical (balanced). Do not strike into the canter until the horse goes perfectly at the trot. Take your time. It is much better to do this exercise three or four times correctly than ten times badly. Keep in mind the importance of precision. Do the same at the walk. Repeat it until the horse does it correctly, then give him a rest as a reward.

B. *The Jumping Exercises.*

1. Cavaletti as usual. Add exercise 5. Also raise the last cavaletti at exercise 4 up to four cavaletti (four feet).
2. The row of fences at the canter.
3. The small course at the canter (parcour) about eight or ten jumps three feet high; at the end of the month up to 12 fences.

Remarks: Now jump three times in the week. Tuesday—do cavaletti and gymnastics on the row of fences at the trot and canter. Thursday—exercise F on approach up to three feet six inches. Saturday—course (parcour).

III STAGE: Fourth Month.

A. *The Ground Work.*

1. The same as was done the previous month.
2. Changing of the lead at the center, with transition to the halt, and
3. Rein Back.
4. Counter canter.
5. Increasing and decreasing of the pace at the gallop.

Remarks: Increasing and decreasing at the gallop, always using the half seat. At the extended trot, always rising (posting). When the horse keeps the pace well at the canter (gallop), drop the reins, and take contact again. Take care that the horse keeps the same pace all the time.

B. *The Jumping Exercises*

The same as was done in the previous month. According to the horse's progress, increase the speed when galloping over fences. Raise the fences occasionally up to three feet six inches. Once in a week jump over a course of 12 fences up to three feet six inches and five feet spread (triple bar). In order to teach the horse obedience to the orders of

Miss A. Lindsey, on her four year old horse at Dyrham Park, England. Even though this was her first show on this horse, the position of her hands and legs is excellent.

("Graphic" Photos)

the rider, include obedience tests in the jumping course.

III STAGE: Fifth Month.
A. *The Ground Work.*
As before. Improving the precision in the reaction to the rider's aids.
B. *The Jumping Exercises.*
As before.

III STAGE: Sixth Month.
A. *The Ground Work.*
The same.
B. *The Jumping Exercises.*
The same.

Example of the lesson in the last two months:
Ground Work:

10 min. walk—extend walk, ordinary walk on contact. Halt, walk, circles and turnings. Turnings on the forehand.

15 min. trot—trot at steady pace, turnings, circles, serpentines, cavaletti; trot, stop, trot. Trot, stop, rein back, trot. Increase and decrease the pace at the trot.

2 - 3 min. rest.

30 min. canter—Free canter in half seat, full seat and start the handiness at the canter—small circles, turnings. First, let us say, to the right, then change the direction and do the same to the left.

1 - 2 min. rest.

Changing from canter to trot and vice versa.
Changing from canter to walk and vice versa.
Changing the leg through halt.
Changing the leg through halt, rein back.

1 - 2 min. rest.

Canter and counter canter.

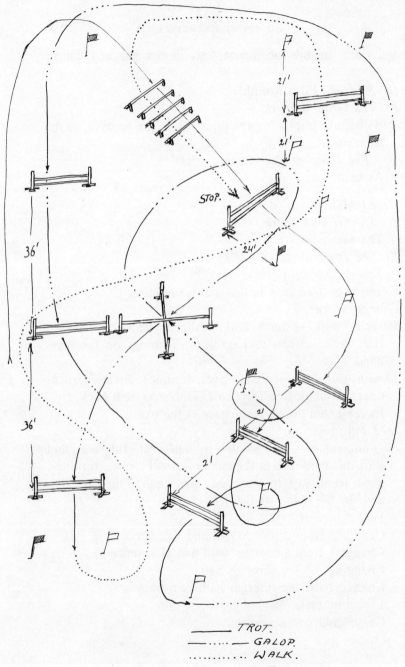

Fig. 49 Example of obedience test.

Increasing and decreasing at canter.

2 - 3 min. extended trot.

5 min. slow trot making sharp turnings and serpentine. Halt.

10 min. walk on loose rein.

Example of Jumping Lesson:

30 min.—loosening work at the walk, trot and canter (canter (canter in half seat) and on cavaletti.

20 min.—Gymnastics on a row of fences at the trot and at the canter. Treating every horse individually, apply the exercises necessary for areas in which the horse needs improvement: style over the fence, or approach, or handiness between the fences.

10 min.—Walk and slow trot, keeping in mind the fact that the horse should finish the work relaxed and calm, and not tired.

Example of an Obedience Test:

The size of the jumps vary according to the stage of training, age, and natural ability of the horse.

Conclusion

As I mentioned in my introduction, I have tried to introduce a method of riding, training the rider and the horse, which one could compare with "basic English," just the necessary knowledge in a simple way.

I have tried to explain the idea of what I think is the modern approach to this subject. Do not take it as "alpha and omega." This is just the first step to the art of equitation. This is sort of a primary school. University comes later.

Still, if you do the preliminary work with the horse and you undergo the preliminary course of riding which I have suggested in this book, you will be able to continue equitation in the correct way without trouble in any direction you wish, i.e., show jumping, cross country riding, or elementary dressage. But, I do not think that there exists a rider who could learn the art of equitation by reading books. One must practice first under the supervision of an experienced instructor. After this, reading books gives valuable help in further improvement and knowledge.

As I said before, there is tremendous interest in riding as a sport. It grows from day to day. Let us hope that the desire for excellence in horsemanship goes with this ever-expanding interest.

Every sport is very valuable, not only for physical development, but also for improving the moral outlook of the human being.

In every sport, competition plays an important part, because it gives an opportunity to compare oneself with others and consequently to improve.

From the educational point of view, team competitions are of much greater value than individual endeavours, because in team work there is no place for egoism. Every member of the team gives his best efforts for the community, be it the team, or the club, or the town, or the country which he represents. It is surprising how this teamwork improves the standard of the individual's best. Teamwork develops friendship, eliminates jealousy, and teaches the members to co-operate in full harmony.

Individual competitions can educate the young competitor, providing he enters in the right spirit. He goes to compete, to compare himself with others, and if he loses, he tries to find out why he was worse than the winner. He should not blame anybody. He should realize that he did something wrong at the moment of competition, or that the others were better-trained or more experienced, or they had better competitive spirit. Individual competitions in riding sport have perhaps more value than in other sports because there the human being co-operates with another living creature, the horse. Together, they form a team; two brains, two spirits, two characters, performing together to the best adavantage for each other. The educational opportunity of this performance is invaluable for a young rider.

During the last twelve years I have trained young riders in four countries. Rather than giving individual lessons, I have always tried to collect my pupils in small groups who are at the same standard of training, to educate them

not only in horsemanship but also towards developing
a competitive spirit and teamwork.

Generally speaking, I have found the parents of my
pupils very helpful and enthusiastic about riding as a sport.
I think that the increased interest in riding is due not only
to the desire to escape from the mechanization of our
times, but to the encouragement given by parents who want
their children to participate in educational and competitive sports.

There are, however, three categories of parents, in my
opinion. In the first category are those who encourage their
children because they understand and appreciate the educational riding as a sport. There is another group who
participate because it seems fashionable at the moment.
The third, alas, are those parents who want the child by
hook or by crook to win, not for the sake of the child but
because of their personal ambitions.

All parents enjoy seeing their children win. This is only
natural. However, the important factor of all competitions
is that the competitor performs well and does his best.
They do not understand that the son or daughter is not
yet ready to win, or has not yet developed the competitive
spirit. They show their disappointment or discontent,
blaming the trainer, the judges, the horse, or something
else which, in their opinion, has interfered with winning.
Naturally, under these conditions, the sport loses its educational value.

I have seen youngsters crying because they did not win.
I had a girl pupil who could not stand others to be better
than she was. When she did not win because she rode badly,
she lost her temper, upset the horse, and finally was elimi-
nated. She cried, did not speak to anybody, and was completely impossible. Her parents considered her to be
another Pat Smythe and spoiled her completely. They did

not realize that Pat Smythe is great not because she knows how to win, but because she knows how to lose. I assure you that she has been defeated as many times as she has won. She is capable of accepting both victory and defeat with the same calmness, dignity, and her usual feminine charm. In my opinion, the British are among the best competitors in the world, because they know how to lose with grace. This is the result of years and years of up-bringing and education in the right sport spirit, which has become part of their tradition.

The following story illustrates my point perfectly. During the Olympic Games in 1936 in Berlin, I watched the 10,000 meter race in the Big Stadium. I do not remember exactly, but I think there were over one hundred competitors from all over the world. There was one young boy, a student from Calcutta, India. He had a black beard and lovely black sad eyes. When he took off his clothes, he looked like Ghandi, he was so thin. "I bet," I said to my friends, "that this 'fakir' will show something terrific. Probably great stamina or speed." The race started. I watched Hindu. He took a certain moderate speed and kept running at this speed all the time, regardless of others, who out-ran him several times. The speed dictated by three Finns and one Japanese competitor was far too fast for him and for many others. Some runners gave up after half the distance of the race; some after three-quarters. But my Hindu kept his same speed without any change. The race finished. Many competitors did not bother even to pass the finish line. My Hindu still ran.

The 280,000 spectators and the judges waited until he accomplished the whole distance. When he finished, the hurricane of applause showed the respect of the public for the boy who had come to the Olympic Games to give his very best effort, which he had done. Everybody applauded as if he had been the winner. This was a wonderful example of Olympic sport spirit. This young boy realized that he could not win, but he did his best, and he learned from experience how much he had to improve.

Do not give up before you have used all your efforts. You will find in everyday life that there are moments when this education in competitive spirit will help you to overcome many difficulties.

I try never to allow my pupils to enter competitions until they are ready. Consequently, I have had the good fortune to train many winners. First comes steady, consistent training and hard work on the part of the pupil. This gives him self-confidence. Then comes the participating in competitions up to the standard of the training. I always ask my riders to ride correctly, using proper style, treating the show as a lesson. After a little experience, winning comes. I never expect my pupils to win when competing for the first time. Do not get swelled-headed when you start to win. Keep being modest and watch others. Listen to their remarks, particularly the older and more experienced riders. Remember that the art of riding, as with all other arts, has no limits to improvement and there is no end to learning.

As a young rider, I met in my country an old gentleman, a famous horseman and horse breeder—Poland's greatest expert in the knowledge of horses. He used to say, "I am not the best judge of horses, as people think I am. Perhaps I make less mistakes than the others because of my life-long experience. But . . . we all make mistakes and we learn until the end of our lives."

I hope that this handful of advice and these remarks will help my readers to find the footpath which will lead them to the highway of success in the art of riding. Although I have spent my lifetime with horses and with people who know and love horses, I find that I have never ceased to learn—this is for me one of the joys of being alive.

Index